GERMANY IN THE GREAT WAR

« MICHAEL GOES TO WAR »
AN ORDINARY GERMAN INFANTRYMAN
1914 -1918

Jean-Claude LAPARRA and Pascal HESSE

Translated from the French by Sally and Lawrence Brown

CONTENTS

HISTOIRE & COLLECTIONS - PARIS

Die Anstifter des Weltkrieges
vor dem Weltgericht.

Prologue
MICHAEL
THE GERMAN INFANTRYMAN 1914-1918

T HE GERMAN ARMY that invaded part of Europe at the beginning of August 1914 was something that was never forgotten by those who saw the passing disciplined columns of infantry, artillery, cavalry, convoys etc.

It gave an impression of strength, solidity and generally of discipline, despite the numerous infamous incidents committed by units or individuals. The first units seen by people were more often those of the regular army. The young, well built men had just been issued with war time uniforms and equipment, their clothing was clean, well cut, even elegant ; the leather was polished and the weapons spotless. The horses were in fine condition, the field kitchens smoking, the smell of the food teasing the appetite of the people in the regions they passed through, wagons and vehicles were in tiptop condition. As a consequence of a war that dragged on, uniforms, equipment and materiel underwent modifications. The outline of the soldier changed, particularly with the adoption of the steel helmet. His appearance also deteriorated ; the mud of the trenches was not solely responsible for this and the economic problems were also felt. At the same time, as for the combatants themselves, and using an expression that they coined themselves, they became

« trench pigs » or « front line pigs » due to the conditions.

In order to show a more complete picture of the German soldier during the Great War, we chose the idea of picking the archetypal infantryman. It did not seem to be wise to successively describe, and in great detail, what made up his uniform, headwear, weapons, personal equipment etc. It seemed more interesting, whilst at the same time having a glimpse of what came before, to show what he did, his environment, food, joy and sadness, behaviour and even his language and so on ; in short, what made up his life. The decision was taken to use the diaries written by an infantryman during the conflict, to re-write them after they were translated into a coherent edited form that is more modern and to include technical information accompanied by a commentary and photographs. These do not have any link with the diaries, they were chosen for educational purposes to illustrate the final text.

The previously mentioned writings were in 12 notebooks. The first was bought on the day the soldier left his garrison. He wrote what he saw, heard and learnt. Alongside personal observations and impressions, he wrote down precise facts and dates, various details as well as the characteristics of certain materiel. He wrote this down chronologically, but not from day to day and in a continuous manner, as if he only consigned to paper that which had caught his attention ; essentially the news that

Michael wearing his cap slightly differently; it bears the cross of the Landwehr (a reminder of the 1813 War of Liberation that was popular in Germany), receives French, Russian and British prisoners, captured guns, the city of Brussels, a « second choice fortress » (Liege) etc. He puts them in boxes that he piles up. An infantryman brings him a sack containing 767,000 French prisoners and 150 guns, saying to him : « Here you are Father Michael, another bag full of old rags to wrap up ! » (Private Collection)

Hier, Vater Michel wieder einen Sack voll Lumpen zum einpacken!

1914

Michael, wearing his characteristic cap, receives on a plate the declarations of war against Germany, at his feet, four German soldiers and a sailor settle the score with Allied representatives, a French « Pioupiou », John Bull, a « Jass » (the Belgian soldier's nickname), a moujik and a Japanese officer. (J-C. Laparra Collection)

reached him of his close family, his life as a soldier and his environment. He wrote little about operations and fighting. When this notebook was full, he managed to send it to his parents. He then bought more which he also managed to save, no doubt miraculously, by sending them home. If we look at the dates, there are only two missing, each one corresponding approximately to a period of three months (Autumn 1917 and Spring 1918). Pages are also missing in the booklets from the spring and autumn of 1916.

These documents were found in a flea market at the Charlottenburg Gate in Berlin in 1999 and are written in a fairly easy to read gothic script. Particularly rich in information, they have one frustrating particularity; they have no usable surname or Christian name and very few indications of whereabouts. Details are missing that would enable the identification of the writer's unit and nationality, that is to say his state, the German Empire being made up of 24 states and four kingdoms (Prussia, Bavaria, Württemberg, Saxe), five great duchies, six duchies, six principalities and three free towns. We only know that he belonged to a regular infantry regiment whose men were musketeers ; different regiments designated an infantryman in this way or as a grenadier, fusilier or *Infanterist*. Perhaps the author of these diaries did not want to get into trouble in the eventuality of the notebooks being found by someone, a superior or being intercepted when sent to his family ? A more plausible explanation, which does not exclude the first, is that he thought he would recover them at a later date, finish them and write his wartime memoirs.

The careful study of the notebooks leads us to consider that this person is emblematic of what the German infantryman was, in a general way, on the Western Front. The reader in this book will follow this unknown soldier, from the moment he left for the war to just before the end of hostilities ; the last notebook ends on 21 October 1918, even though there are blank pages. What happened to the writer and how did this notebook join the others ? We will never know.

Michael is the name we have given to this unknown soldier. Why this name ? The « German Michael » *(Deutsher Michael)* an old character of German political caricature, is a stereotype. He is the national personification of the German people, destined to represent the spirit of those who are subject to the powers that be and their excesses. Without corresponding exactly, he is the equivalent of Marianne for France, John Bull for Great Britain and Uncle Sam for the United States. The character of Michael, testified since 911, is supposed to be initially derived from the Archangel Saint Michael, patron saint and protector of the German people. He has really been known since the XVI century with the appearance of a slightly sleepy countryman wearing a hat similar to a nightcap.

Evolving throughout the centuries, he really became the incarnation of some of the Germans during the period known as *Vormärz* (1830-1848). Until the Great War, he was the symbol, in the social democratic press, of national unity as well as the people under an authoritarian government

Neue Kriegslieder

Musik für ALLE

Preis 50 Pf (60 h)

and somewhat kindly. After November 1918, he represented the guiltless victims in the face of the victors' demands.

In the meantime, Saint Michael is still called upon ; the Archangel lent his name, in 1917, to the fortified line protecting the bottom of the Saint-Mihiel salient (that is to say, defending the west/south west access to Metz) and, in 1918, to the offensive on the Somme and in Picardy from 21 March to 4 April.

THE RE-WRITTEN NOTEBOOKS

INFANTRYMAN MICHAEL'S WAR

On 31 July 1914, a heavy atmosphere lay over the country ; the state of possible war was declared at 12 o'clock, with notably the call up of certain categories of reservists. In the small town where he lived, Michael saw serious and upset faces all around him. The son of a printer, the eldest of six children, he went to his district's primary school. He then worked with his father until called up for his military service. With this service completed, he found work as a typesetter for a newspaper. His military obligations were fulfilled from 1911 to 1913, only two years as Michael served in the infantry. Given his excellent physical fitness, he has been incorporated and not put in the replacement reserve (Ersatzreserve). Released from service the year before, he has not yet been called up for exercises as a reservist. With the announcement that war is imminent, Michael knows that he will be mobilised. His father won't be. In the spring of this year, he has reached the age limit for being called

Above.
A large size collection
of 15 « War Songs »,
published in the popular
« Music for all » collection
by Ullstein (Berlin and
Vienna). Each of these is
presented in the same way
as the picture shown here
opposite.
(J-C. Laparra Collection)

and representing a class-structured imperialism. Obviously, the character, who up to that point was neither militaristic nor warlike, suffered a little from his negative side, his somewhat half asleep appearance, in the literal as well as the figurative sense, hence the call « Wake up Michael ! ».

From August 1914, he symbolises the patriotic union : although « German Michael » is a « good Michael », full of a great desire for peace, he is still capable of fighting when necessary. In a book of songs published at the beginning of the conflict, one of the songs is called « To Michael, war song in low German ». The phrase « You, German Michael » is repeated twice and he is encouraged to carry out his duty against the enemies of his country. Wearing a uniform, Michael becomes the symbol of a Germany at war, and so of the German soldier at the Front. He still remains a humorous character

One of the songs in the book « To Michael,
a war song in low German ». (J-C. Laparra Collection)

Wilhelm II, religion and war

Wilhelm II made Bismark's formula his own: « In dark times, we Germans fear God but nothing else in this world! ». For the monarch of divine right that he claimed to be, the armed forces and the imperial navy were his ultima ratio regum. Holding the Roman emperor Constantine, the real organiser of Christianity, in high regard, this worship expressed itself in religion as well as the arts.

The imperial standard (Labarum), made on the orders of Constantine, was of a special interest in his eyes, as, according to a tradition, it was of divine inspiration. On the eve of the Battle of Milvius Bridge, that opened to him the gates of Rome in 312, Constantine is supposed to have seen a cross in the sky, accompanied by the inscription « In hoc signo vinces » (By this sign you will win). He painted crosses on his standards and won

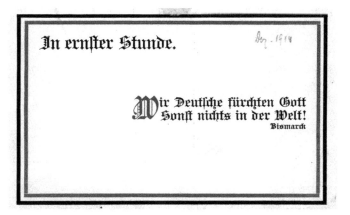

In ernster Stunde.

Dez. 1914

Wir Deutsche fürchten Gott
Sonst nichts in der Welt!
Bismarck

the battle. The Labarum in this way legitimised the power of Constantine. By referring to this, the Kaiser wished to become part of the lineage of the sovereigns chosen by God and ordered two copies of this standard, one for Pope Pius X and one for himself.

He also particularly worshipped Saint Michael, patron of the German people, protector of Germany and even Europe. In his eyes, the Archangel symbolised the political objectives that he pursued and the emperor liked that, in his artistic representations, for his own likeness to be given to him. For example, in 1901, on a painting by Max Gärtner, he portrayed him additionally wearing the distinctive markings of the Teutonic knights and a shield painted in the three colours of Germany, upon which stood out an imperial eagle.
(J-C. Laparra Collection)

up into the territorial branch (Landsturm 2nd edict). He is, therefore, free from his military obligations.

The next day sees the appearance of the imperial decree for mobilisation on the 2nd. Michael knows what the mobilisation orders entail that have been delivered by the recruitment office where he has been registered since the end of his military service. He knows that on the 2nd he will have to join his unit.

2 AUGUST 1914.
MICHAEL IS MOBILISED

Michael leaves his parents' home early in the morning. He did not want his parents to come with him to the station so that leaving would not be made more difficult and

The last formality for men released from military service before leaving the barracks, the « Hurra for the Emperor ! » on the incitation of an officer.
(Das Kleine Buch vom Deutschen Heere, 1901)

A barrack room souvenir photo.
Comrades about to be released from their military service proudly display their reservist pipes, decorated with regimental mementos. The full equipment of the perfect reservist comprised the pipe, beer stein, water bottle, walking stick, large cup and saucer etc. These objects were bought at the barrack's canteen or at specialist outlets.
(Private Collection)

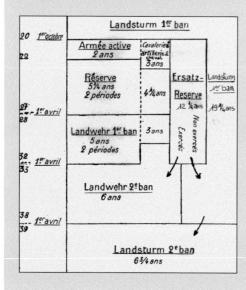

The portrait of Wilhelm II on the body of a reservist pipe.
(J-C. Laparra Collection)

The back of the pipe carries the inscription « A memento of my military service. »
(J-C. Laparra Collection)

The organisation of recruitment

The *Ersatzreserve* was a category of reservists where the men would remain for 12 years (from 20 to 32 years). This is explained by the boom in German births in the decades before the war. The drafting of the whole contingent was impossible due to budgetary reasons.

Each year, 80,000 to 100,000 men deemed fit for service were not called up for normal service. They only had to undergo three periods of training for a total duration of 20 weeks.

From the beginning of August 1914, 250,000 men in this category were incorporated and rapidly trained. (P. Hesse Collection)

mental recruit depot. Given the year of his class, he will rejoin his regiment with the reinforcements that will replace losses. He is issued with various items of clothing and equipment which, in total, comprise

so that he would not see his mother upset. On the platform, he sees other young men from his hometown. He knows some of them. The general atmosphere is rather happy ; everyone, soldiers, the mobilised, men and women do not doubt in the slightest Germany's right to declare war and feel that they have to take part in the defence of their homeland, that is, in their eyes, under threat. Many jokes are made. The journey to the closest large town passed quickly as the time was spent joking, laughing and singing. Michael and his new comrades make their way to the barracks through streets adorned with flags and filled with the patriotic population ; the barracks are well known to them as they spent two years here. Upon arrival, they find mostly reserve officers and NCOs, all from the region. The few regular officers present are relatively old, some had already been attached to the regiment from 1911 to 1913.

At the end of July, the regiment was on manoeuvres in a camp, the officers, NCOs and other ranks still wore the dark blue uniform. The unit was informed during the night of the 29th-30th that it had to rejoin its garrison. The 2nd, when Michael arrives at the barracks at the end of the morning, his regiment has just left as part of the first concentration movements.

After the formalities of incorporation, followed by a basic lunch, Michael is attached to a company of a replacement battalion (*Ersatzbattaillon*) of his regi-

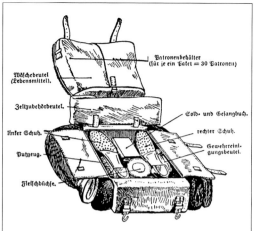

1914 headwear: between tradition and modernity

For certain tasks, or when he is not on service, Michael wears a round field cap in the same colour as the uniform. In the infantry, the service and campaign headwear remains the model 1895 spiked helmet, as in peacetime.

Fitted with a fabric cover for camouflage reasons, this has the regimental number stitched to the front. The numbers were cut from cloth or red felt. The helmet is made from boiled leather which is then covered in black varnish.

A brass strip goes from the base of the spike to the rear peak and offers the head mediocre protection. The spike and its base, decorative and protective elements, but nonetheless a nuisance, give an old fashioned look to this helmet. A frontal plate represents a heraldic emblem and varies according to state and sometimes regiments.

Given imperial Germany's diversity and even that of regions that make up Prussia, this helmet is considered by many Germans as the symbol of Prussian militarism.

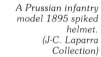

The queue for meals at a regimental recruitment depot.
The men are lined up to receive their meals in an individual mess tin, made from iron in the shape of a small basin.
This was not taken on campaign.
They wear their dark blue uniforms; the usual tunic could be replaced by an old model dark grey Litewka.
(Stegmann/Baur Collection)

A Prussian infantry model 1895 spiked helmet.
(J.-C. Laparra Collection)

Opposite. Two examples of the same model. The one on the left has an eagle bearing the banner and inscription « With God for the King and the Fatherland » as well as the initials FR (Fredericus Rex) and two barely visible cockades (towards the left that of the Empire: black, white, red; towards the right that of Prussia: black, white, black. The helmet on the right is the same as the previous one with its cover. The red numbers, taken off after 15 August 1914 and not replaced with green equivalents, have been drawn on in ink.
(J.-C. Laparra Collection)

« Demob in... »
A postcard written by a man at Morhange, to another Lorraine man serving in the Imperial Navy (S.M.S. Braunschweig). It talks of the number of days left for the sender before the end of his military service.
« The watchword is going home! For the reserve there is still: Months, Days, Bread (number of – to receive) and Money (outstanding pay) ».
(J.-C. Laparra Collection)

the following kit : a tunic and trousers, neck cloth, two shirts, greatcoat, two pairs of socks, underwear, a round, peakless field cap (Mütze), nicknamed the « head scratcher », a spiked helmet and its cover, a pair of marching boots and strong socks, a belt with a brass buckle with emblem, bayonet frog and a false knot, two ammunition pouches, a backpack made from strong canvas with a brown fur covered flap (fur on the outside), a tent section with its accessories, blanket, haversack (literally bread bag) and its strap, a water bottle and its cover, an individual field mess tin, folding cutlery, individual tool, and a set of twill uniform (normally used for certain tasks).

Michael is provisionally issued with a walking out tunic and trousers. The two main garments that make up this uniform are in dark blue (dunkelblau). This uniform is not really suited for modern war and is kept as a walking out or parades, as well as for garrison service and training.

A few days after being issued with his uniform, Michael is given, for everyday use, an old model dark grey tunic (Litewka), in exchange for the corresponding dark blue tunic. The feldgrau uniform will only be issued just before leaving the garrison and going on campaign. The pair of boots are the old model 1866 in fawn coloured leather ;

An das Deutsche Volk.

Seit der Reichsgründung ist es durch 43 Jahre Mein und Meiner Vorfahren heißes Bemühen gewesen, der Welt den Frieden zu erhalten und im Frieden unsere kraftvolle Entwickelung zu fördern. Aber die Gegner neiden uns den Erfolg unserer Arbeit.

Alle offenkundige und heimliche Feindschaft von Ost und West, von jenseits der See haben wir bisher ertragen im Bewußtsein unserer Verantwortung und Kraft. Nun aber will man uns demütigen. Man verlangt, daß wir mit verschränkten Armen zusehen, wie unsere Feinde sich zu tückischem Überfall rüsten, man will nicht dulden, daß wir in entschlossener Treue zu unserem Bundesgenossen stehen, der um sein Ansehen als Großmacht kämpft und mit dessen Erniedrigung auch unsere Macht und Ehre verloren ist.

So muß denn das Schwert entscheiden. Mitten im Frieden überfällt uns der Feind. Darum auf! zu den Waffen! Jedes Schwanken, jedes Zögern wäre Verrat am Vaterlande.

Um Sein oder Nichtsein unseres Reiches handelt es, daß unsere Väter neu sich gründeten. Um Sein oder Nichtsein deutscher Macht und deutschen Wesens. Wir werden uns wehren bis zum letzten Hauch von Mann und Roß. Und wir werden diesen Kampf bestehen auch gegen eine Welt von Feinden. Noch nie ward Deutschland überwunden, wenn es einig war.

Vorwärts mit Gott, der mit uns sein wird, wie er mit den Vätern war.

Berlin, den 6. August 1914.

Wilhelm.

the well worn ankle boots are still the old model with side laces. The leather items (belt, ammunition pouches, backpack straps) are in fawn coloured leather. Luckily, the unit to which Michael belongs has not been issued with the old white parade leather equipment that would have to be blackened. The two ammunition pouches are the model 1909. Adopted on 26 January 1910, they are made from thick, very light fawn leather, that will darken with use. Each pouch has three compartments, each one with four five round clips, for a total of 60 per pouch.

Some of Michael's comrades have been issued with the previous model 1895 pouches, that will remain in service throughout the conflict. As for the water bottle, a clip attaches it to the model 1887 bread bag, attached to the belt on the right rear hand side of the body, which is why it was known as the « arse knocker ». At this time, the water bottle is the aluminium model 1907, with a grey-brown or grey-green cloth cover. The individual model

The model 1898 rifle

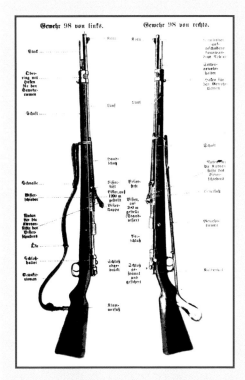

The standard weapon issued throughout the duration of the war was the model 1898 Mauser, 1.250 m in length and weighing 4.100 kg.

It fired modern and efficient ammunition, the 7.92 mm model 1904 cartridge with the S bullet (Spitzgeschoss, pointed bullet).

A repetition weapon with a five round magazine loaded with clips, this excellent rifle was equipped with a model 1898 n.A. (neuer Art: new model) bayonet, with flat blade and wooden grips.

This bayonet was 51.5 cm in length and weighed 0.430 kg. Its leather scabbard was worn on the belt and secured by a frog, from which hung a false knot in company and battalion colours.

(Dilthey's militärischer Dienst-Unterricht für Einjährig-Freiwillige, 1906)

1910 mess tin in blackened aluminium and the brown model 1892 tent section are attached to the backpack. The tent accessories, a model 1892 pull string, model 1901 poles, two wood and iron model 1901 tent pegs, in their canvas model 1892 bag and spare rations, are packed inside. Provisionally, Michael is issued with a sort of large bowl made from tin. His equipment also comprises of a model 1874 entrenching tool, one of the personal tools issued to soldiers that is part of the campaign equipment. This is held in a carrier attached to the belt on the left hand side. The entrenching tool handle, at thigh level, is attached to the bayonet scabbard to avoid them banging together.

In the meantime, on 4 August, the Reichstag, the legislative chamber that incarnates the will of the German states, has agreed to the decision taken by Wilhelm II, pla-cing the fate of his people in the outcome of the conflict. On the 6th, Wilhelm II, the « Warlord », issues two proclamations ; one addresses his army and navy, the other the German people.

In the weeks that follow, Michael is at his regimental depot and his daily tasks are uninteresting. His timetable initially consists of the induction of new arrivals and training has to be undertaken again. Appearance, saluting, drill. The rifles are not all of the most recent type, some are old. It is funny to see how they are so clumsily held by some. The mobilised men are also submitted to several marches with full equipment, destined to get them used once more to long distances on foot. The captain commanding the company of recruits to which Michael belongs sometimes gallops alongside the column. When he arrives at the head, the men march past and he shouts : « Any man who has undone his collar will carry a second rifle. »

One day, Michael has to give his rifle to the man next to him who has been spotted for his slovenliness. The lieutenant tries to defend the man in question, but the captain replies : « No collar hook will be unfastened without permission. Where would the army be if everyone did what they wanted ? Stop being so soft. I know what men can endure ! »

During this period, there is only one target practice session with the standard issue rifle, the model 1898 Mauser.

Some examples of markings on personal items. From top to bottom. Three examples on a great coat, then on a tunic, underwear and another item.
(J-C. Laparra Collection)

The feldgrau uniform has just been issued to an infantryman of a Württemberg reserve regiment. The man has let his trouser legs fall over his boots according to a custom which is attributed to the Saxons. He is armed with a model 1898 rifle and the model 1898 n.A. bayonet. With his pack on his back and a small bouquet in between two button holes, he strikes the traditional pose of a recruit about to go on campaign.
(P. Hesse Collection)

Feldgrau. *The German equivalent of khaki*

Introduced by the order of the imperial cabinet of 14 February 1907, the War Ministry order of 19 April 1907, the decree of 23 February 1910 and the application orders of 18 March 1910, a feldgrau uniform was adopted for the whole army for all units, ranks and branches.

In 1914, all regular units had been issued with the model 1907/10 uniform, with one set per man, kept in stores and only worn when on manoeuvres or campaign.

The model 1907/10 feldgrau cloth tunic (Feldrock) was identical in appearance to the model 1895 (Waffenrock) but with a turn down collar. It was cotton lined and closed at the front by eight buttons as well as a collar hook. The two large exterior pockets had a flap

secured by a button. For the tunic and the greatcoat, there was only one pair of shoulder straps in feldgrau cloth, the coloured type for the dark blue uniform was not taken on campaign. The trousers were also feldgrau.

The greatcoat was still the 1901 model in light bluish grey cloth, with a cotton hood that folded into pocket secured by a button.

There was also a model 1907 greatcoat, almost identical in cut but without a hood, made in a slightly darker cloth than the previous model. The collar, designed to be turned up and fastened with a loop, did not always have the rectangular patches taken off to make the soldier less conspicuous.

NCOs and infantrymen of different army corps

| Grenadier | Bugler | Adjutant (Feldwebel) | Infantryman | Machine gunner (machine gun detachment) | Light Infantry | Stretcher bearer | NCO between Corporal and Sergeant (Unteroffizier) |

(Die graue Felduniform der Deutschen Armee, 1910).

There are, however, plenty of cleaning jobs to be done after the departure of the regular regiment, so that the barrack rooms will be ready to receive the men mobilised for a *Landwehr* regiment. In the canteen, a photographer with authorisation from the superiors, sometimes comes to take group photos. It is not rare for some of the groups to place a sign in front with inscriptions such as : « *Who knows if we'll come back.* » The atmosphere is a happy one though, because the newspapers are publishing reports that the advance in the west, that is the Schlieffen Plan, is meeting almost no resistance.

On 22 August, part of the *Ersatz* battalion to which Michael belongs, is called to the quarter master's store. The fact that the *feldgrau* uniform is issued, means that the men who receive it are going to join the regiment at the Front. Later, when the atmosphere of patriotic fever has fallen,

the recruits who receive this new uniform nickname it the « mortuary suit ». Michael is lucky, as since the quartermaster is from his town, he manages to change his old pair of model 1893 boots with their side laces, for a more modern model with frontal laces (model 1901). These new boots, in natural colour leather, will need breaking in by being worn even when not on service. After the issuing of these uniforms, the same authorised photographer waits in a room for those who wish to have their photograph taken in order to send a last picture of themselves to their families. The pose is struck in a conventional way, with the full campaign equipment of helmet, pack, rifle, and a small bunch of flowers placed in a button hole or slid between two buttons, as if it is the day of departure.

Michael has not been able to go and see his parents since mobilisation. He wrote to say goodbye and received

Pay books

In the barrack courtyard, every soldier about to depart receives his Soldbuch. The box on the right contains the two types of books. On the left is the Soldbuch, on the right the Militärpass. (Grosser Bilder-Atlas des Weltkrieges, 1915).

The Soldbuch is sometimes protected by a thick, stiff cardboard cover, bought in the canteen and decorated with a motif that is a reminder of the unit (name, number, crest etc.). On the last page of the pay book is pasted a list of items that make up the full kit.

The military book (Militärpass) is filed away at the company office (reservists keep it at home and a mobilisation order is pasted inside), and is used to note down all things that correspond to military career of the holder; rank, surname, Christian name, wife's name and those of the parents, controls by the

Each soldier has two pay books issued by the unit where he was initially incorporated.

The pay book (Soldbuch), taken on campaign, is carried, according to regulations, in a pocket made for it on the left hand side of the chest. It can also be stored in the backpack. The Soldbuch successively contains : several elements that permit identification and summary filiation, successive postings with the soldier's number within the company, physical characteristics, shoe size, vaccinations, periods of hospitalisation (with items received at this time and personal items held), pay received, bonuses or allowances etc.

recruitment service and successive addresses (for reservists), civil status, profession, religion, unit of incorporation, service number in this company, successive campaigns (units, dates of battles in which the holder participated), convocations or exercises (for reservists), etc.

their reply on the day of departure. He has learnt that his first brother, aged 19, has just enlisted for the duration of the war without waiting to be called up with his class. He is going to stay at home for a few weeks before being called up which will happen at the end of August. His mother, who wrote the letter, ended by hoping that he would behave well and stay healthy. Having folded the envelope and slid it into his wallet, Michael goes to the canteen (Kantine) to buy some letter paper. Men are running in the corridors. At the canteen, some are buying basic necessities, particularly foot cream. Some soldiers, standing at the counter, are drinking brandy and making jokes at the expense of the French. Others remain silent and deep in thought. Michael sees some small linen backed notebooks. He asks for one with the idea of writing down his thoughts when he has a quiet moment. Going to war is an experience that he would no doubt like to remember later.

The time to leave approaches. Michel has a little tummy trouble, no doubt a consequence of worry as to what awaits, and has to go to the latrines. He then shoulders his heavy pack and goes down into the courtyard. The unit to which he belongs, forming a company, lines up

under the orders of the *Spiess,* the slang term for the company adjutant, the *Feldwebel. Spiess* means spear, dagger, brooch ; indeed, the adjutant is a senior NCO equipped with a sabre, in German military vocabulary, he is a *Porte Epee.*

Soldbuch and Militärpass. *(J-C. Laparra Collection)*

Instructions from a cream to protect feet from overheating, destined for the military.
(J-C. Laparra Collection)

This postcard portrays the departure of a reservist father of four children, without doubt a man of the Landwehr (an allusion to the War of Liberation of 1813). The scene is accompanied by part of a popular song, written at the end of the XIX century by Hugo Zuschneid, exalting leaving on campaign.
1st verse
« Now is the time to leave,
we are going on campaign.
We want to march quickly
And bravely use our weapons. »
Chorus
« Glory, glory, victory!
With our heart and hands for the Fatherland!
The birds in the forest Sing wonderfully.
To home, to home.
We say See you again'! »
(J-C. Laparra Collection)

For the occasion, the *Feldwebel* carries his sabre, thus showing that he is a *Porte Epee* NCO. From here, the men queue up for the armoury where they will receive a new Mauser rifle with its bayonet. When back in the courtyard, small bunches of flowers, brought in from outside, are handed out to the men who attach them to a button on their chest. Some manage to hang them onto the helmet cover, near the spike.

One last formality takes place; line after line, the men present themselves, when their name is called out in front of a table where a senior sergeant gives them their pay book. The parade is over, the men make a last check of their belt and everything that hangs from it, ammunition pouches, bayonet, bread bag, backpack and so on, as well as other items of equipment. The company parades perfectly and is inspected by the major in command of the depot. There is no religious ceremony for this departure, as was the case when the regiment left on 2 August. The commander just addresses the men with fiery encouragement.

In the barrack courtyard, equipment is checked one last time.
(Grosser Bilder-Atlas des Weltkrieges, 1915)

Recruits awaiting the arrival of the train that will take them to the Front. (J.-C. Laparra Collection)

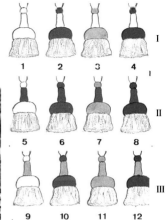

Bayonet knots

The colours enabled the identification of battalions (I, II, III) and the companies (1 to 12) in each infantry regiment. For the machine guns, the colours were white, light blue, white.

Unit identification

Helmet plates with the state coats of arms.
(Private Collection)

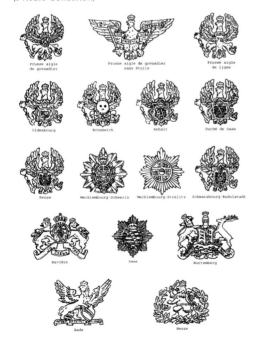

Belt buckles.
(Private Collection)

Greatcoat, dress tunic and tunic buttons. (Private Collection)

END OF AUGUST 1914.
MICHAEL LEAVES
FOR THE WEST

Fredericus Rex

This name corresponds to the king of Prussia Frederick II, called Frederick the Great and named affectionately «Old Fritz» (1712 - 1786). Simultaneously he was Frederick IV of Brandenburg and Frederick II of Prussia. He was the third king in Prussia (1740-1772) then first king of Prussia (from 1772 to the time of his death). A philosopher king and an «enlightened despot», he made his country a great European power. He introduced the initials FR into Prussian military symbolism. These initials are notably seen on eagles decorating certain Prussian headwear.

« *Company, attention! By platoons, on the right, quick march! Halt! Company, forward, quick march!* »

A band from another barracks plays « *Fredericus Rex (King Frederick), our king and master* ». The cymbals and the bass drum echo all over the parade ground. The company marches on. Michael is at the front, with the first platoon. In front of him is a lieutenant carrying a small varnished leather haversack like a school bag. The heels with their inverted horseshoes and the hobnailed soles make a vigorous and determined sound on the cobblestones.

In front of the barracks' gates, the massed crowd moves aside and cheers the departing men who cross the town to the station, intoxicated by the shouts and encouragements, sometimes covered by a rain of roses. It has to be said that the German soldier is an admirable sight at the beginning of the war. The newly designed uniform is worn in an almost identical manner in front line units. With practical equipment and tried and tested weaponry, he is on a par with his British counterpart amongst the men the most apt to go on campaign.

Under the railway bridge, the brass and cymbals boom out. Upon arriving in the yard of the goods station, the soldiers place their packs on the ground. Some Red Cross women pass with flower decorated baskets and hand out bread and chocolate. The train is coming. « *Company, to your rifles! Pick up your packs and rifles!* » The unit is commanded by officers and NCOs who are also part of the reinforcements, and is led onto the platform. The train moves slowly, and is made up of goods wagons, a third class wagon for the officers and senior NCOs, plus some flat cars carrying various equipment. At the command « *to the wagons* », the men surge forward and clamber into the wagons that are fitted with backless benches for the men to sit on. It is all about grabbing the best places. Michael is in no hurry. The doors are closed, or more exactly, left slightly open, the men within not wanting to be completely closed in cattle trucks. Finally, the engine whistles and the train moves off.

The train next stops in three stations, each stop allowing the embarkation of 150 to 200 soldiers, perhaps reinforcements for other units of the Division. At the last stop, the train is full. Each station sees the handing out of fruit, chocolate, bread rolls and even postcards. Going through some stations, the train slows down enough, for a few seconds, to wave or exchange a few words with members of their family who have come to watch the train pass by. Where are we going? Most think it will be Russia. By the doors, some sing patriotic songs, notably the « *Song of Germans* » in which the third verse starts by « *Deutschland über alles* ». There are also more melancholy songs. Mouth organs play popular tunes. Most of the names of the train stations that are passed through point to the West. Two days of travelling, spent singing, sleeping and kneeling down playing scat.

From time to time, the train stops in a station with a food distribution point run by members of the Red Cross. They hand out hot food through the open wagon doors and distribute sweets, cigarettes, letter paper pencils and so on. Naturally, the youngest female volunteers are very popular with the soldiers. It is also the moment to run to the latrines. A field kitchen has also been set up on a flat

Red Cross helpers (Freiwillige Krankenpflege) hand out drinks to the troops passing through the station. (P. Hesse Collection)

car and the men can have their cups or water bottles filled with hot coffee. In a station, the men, holding their mess tins, form a queue in order to be led into a large hut. Behind a table, women serve beef and pasta. All this takes place under the gaze of an elderly man with slightly long white hair. He wears the uniform of a colonel and walks up and down, no doubt a former officer who has been brought back into service as a station commander at the time of the mobilisation.

The Rhine is crossed at night. Searchlights search the sky for possible enemy aircraft or airships. Despite the noise, Michael can hear the men of a nearby wagon singing « Watch on the Rhine » at the top of their voices. This veritably warlike patriotic song is also sung by Michael and his comrades. The journey continues and the Belgian border is crossed. A few hours later, the men climb off the train. A provisional battalion is made up from the four units transported on the train. « Form fours! » The pack, ammunition and rifle are as heavy as lead, even more so given the uncomfortable, noisy and tiring journey. To top it all, they have to sing, as the order « Sing! » has been given. Successively heard, therefore, are « God, Emperor and Fatherland », the « Song of the flags of Germany » and the « Hussars' song ». At the sight of a grave containing several soldiers, with its freshly turned earth, the men spontaneously sing:

« Dry your tears Louise,
Wipe your eyes,
Despite the bullets Louise,
I'll die an old man! »

The smell of sweaty bodies wafts through the ranks, generated by the slightly water proof effect of the uniform. The battalion passes by, relatively quickly, fields, meadows, woods, streams and bridges. Generally speaking, the crops are still standing in the fields or partially harvested, some in stacks, some cut but scattered. Sometimes, on each side of the road, traces of earlier fighting can be seen. Trampled fields, shell holes, abandoned equipment and putrefying corpses that give off a disgusting and stomach churning smell.

There are some civilians, watched over by German soldiers with shouldered rifles, but with fixed bayonets, collecting bodies, dragging them along with long hooks, in order to carry out mass burials in hastily dug pits. Another hour's march and the battalion arrives in a village where the war has caused damage to the roofs, walls, doors, windows and fences. Acrid fumes waft through the streets dominated by the smell of burning. The men are billeted in various barns, exhausted by the conditions of the journey, the fatigue of the march and the heat. Some ask if they can take off and dry their sweat soaked uniforms.

MICHAEL AND THE MARCH FORWARD

The following morning, reveille is sounded. « Here comes the field kitchen! » The barns fill with half clothed men who go and get some coffee and a piece of bread. There is hardly enough time to eat this frugal breakfast before the order is given to strap up the packs. The distribution of reinforcements is carried out by the adjutants, along with much barking out. A detail surprises Michael; they are at war, but, like at the barracks, the Feldwebel carry their large black note book, slid between two buttons of their tunic. This well known note book is used to write down

orders read out on parade and also the punishments handed out. Along with ten others like himself, including his « locker comrade » and a room mate, Michael is detailed to a company. All are taken in front of the captain commanding the company that Michael recognizes as the son of a rich bourgeois family from the regimental recruiting zone. He was a lieutenant in the company where Michael finished his military service. When Michael's turn comes to introduce himself, he takes the liberty of adding to regulation formula a brief mention of this time, said in a way that does not drop the usage of the third person. The officer replies with a few kind words.

A field kitchen placed on a train to keep the troops on board fed when halted in a station. (J-C. Laparra Coll.)

The smell of the German soldier

« "An unbearable smell of sweat and tallow, grabbed my throat, the characteristic smell of the wounded German soldier, caused by water proof qualities of his clothing, that trapped sweat " (p. 200). This is the only attempt at a scientific explanation of a phenomenon mentioned by nearly all of the writers at the Front and attributed by some, the fanatics, to the bestial nature of the German. »

(Bernard A., in CRU J.-N. Témoins. Veteran first hand accounts collated and published from 1915 to 1928. PUN, 1993. p. 92)

Working on field fortifications

During offensive or defensive movements, the infantrymen could be called upon to make a temporary halt.

They would then have to take protective measures. They also had to dig in, under enemy fire, on the line reached. In the prone position, they made scrapes to shoot from.

Working in pairs, they helped each other with their entrenching tools so that whilst one man dug, the other could shoot.

These scrapes were deepened in order to shoot standing up. These isolated holes were then linked up to form a continuous fire trench.

(Information gathered from the war relative to field fortifications. June 1915. German document translated by the S.T.G., 1915.)

A battalion marches towards the enemy. This is made up of three waves; each one certainly of one company (the position of the fourth cannot be made out). The first is no doubt in columns of platoons, the second by platoons joined together with a gap between them, the third in lines of platoons. (Private Collection)

The regiment is now at full wartime strength. Its commander decided to make the most of some spare time so that the company commanders can (re)take their subordinates in hand. Apart from the fact that they are all from the same region, they will bond together through the rigorous carrying out of platoon and company exercises, finishing up with a tactical evolution on the level of each battalion. Demonstrations of digging individual holes is even carried out so that each man, including the new draft, know the techniques of field fortification.

The following day, when the coffee is being distributed, the adjutant shouts to the men « *Today, in principle, is a rest day! Do what you want but stay here!* »

Behind the farm where Michael's platoon is billeted, there is a canal. When the day grows hotter, many of the men go there. They undress, leaving their clothes on the grass under the sun, then stark naked, jump into the water. The canal is deep but the water flows slowly. In a nearby meadow, some play chase.

A parade is announced. They have to get dressed again. It is the regimental paymaster officer, who, to distribute the pay, goes around the companies. Michael's company is grouped together then organised into a long line that passes in front of a table, upon which are placed documents and bags containing bank notes and coins. The paymaster officer sits behind the table along with two NCOs. Each man passes in front of the table, gives his name and holds out his pay book. The money paid is quickly written down in the pay book. When the paymaster and his men are gone, the men are dismissed and everyone heads to a covered cart nearby. This is the regimental canteen cart which also goes from company to company. Anything of interest has already been sold, all that is left is letter paper and polish.

In the afternoon, instead of the continuation of the rest period, the Regiment is paraded. The thirteen companies (three battalions of four companies plus that of the machine guns) form a large U shape in a meadow for a church service. The officers stand in front of their units. A chaplain on horseback arrives with the colonel in command of the regiment. He wears boots and a grey uniform with purple collar facings, and a sort of soft cap or horse riding hat with upturned edges. On his chest, a silver cross hangs from a chain. The chaplain goes to the centre of the U and gives a sermon that ends with an expression and a blessing. His voice is not loud enough, and Michael, under the effect of the heat and fatigue, has not heard much. All that he has heard at two different moments are the following principles, one being that the rights and laws are the columns upon which rest the state, the other is that it is sweet and fitting to die for one's country. When dismissed, Michael's company goes back to the part of the village where they are billeted. The next day, the regiment enters France; upon crossing the border, Michael sees that his battalion's flag is flying; then, like the others, the company shouts a triple « hurrah ! » at the moment they march in front of the barrier.

On September 1, Michael notes that his company has not been given any bread for several days. At midday and in the evening, the meal is the same, bits of meat floating in a hot, greasy stock. Who would have the time to peel vegetables when the advance halts late in the evening, the exhausted men falling into a barn and getting up again at dawn to march once more?

On the 11th of the same month, Michael's company is detailed for a night attack. They have to take the French forward positions by surprise and push them back. The companies are formed up on a road, shielded from view by houses, trees and bushes. The order is given to unload rifles and fix bayonets. The battalion changes from a marching column to company formations which are themselves organised into lines of platoons. They begin to make their way across the fields. Suddenly, in front, rifle fire crackles. Then, « boom ! » Projectiles fall – haphazardly – in the field where the battalion advances. The company commander gives the order to deploy as riflemen and continue the advance. By now, bullets are flying. The captain shouts « Forward ! » and the whole mass of his men advance. The rifle fire crackles continuously, but it is impossible to see anything. Finally, the company reaches the edge of a wood, the order is

(J.-C. Laparra Collection)

After an infantry attack

In the foreground, a drummer's snare drum that, no doubt before going into action, sounded the charge.

given to halt and to dig in. The men dig individual holes. On the 20th, at sun rise, the regiment is ready to move, lined up in the main street of a village. The company commander quickly addresses the men to encourage them.

« *Yesterday was a tough day, today might be even harder. So be brave !* »

The regiment moves off. As it advances, the sound of artillery grows louder. Officers and runners pass quickly along the column. Sometimes they are overtaken on the left side of the road by an artillery convoy. When crossing through a forest, the column halts for a rest. Michael sees far off that the battalion flag is flying. The captain mentions this to his men and says that, no doubt the battalion is going to march into action.

It is true ; orders are shouted out and the three battalions separate in order to advance in company columns. Michael's company progresses across country by mea-

The first changes to the uniforms

From the beginning of the conflict, the campaign uniform underwent a few changes. On 15 August 1914, a decree from the War Ministry stipulated that, from now on the tunic should be closer fitting. The facings were simplified, although they were bigger, they just had a lapel. The false flaps of the skirts disappeared. The shade of feldgrau was darker and also greener than that of the previous model. The trousers were no longer grey-green but stone grey ; the change in colour was justified by the need for economy and feldgrau faded too quickly when washed or in the sunlight. These new items of uniform only appeared at the Front at the beginning of 1915.

Ich hatt' einen Kameraden

« *I had a comrade You wouldn't find a better one. The drum beat the charge, He marched at my side. With the same step and speed. (repeat)*

A bullet comes towards us, For you or for me ? It took his life, He lay at my feet, As if he was part of me. (repeat)

Did his hand want to touch me, Whilst I was reloading ? I can't take your hand, You are now in eternal life, My good comrade ! » *(repeat)*

(J.-C. Laparra Collection)

The importance of the group

In a trench, the group (a platoon comprises four squads, each with two groups) is the basic defensive unit. The gaps between the groups are covered by the flanking fire from neighbouring groups and the lateral positions. Other defences are also set up in the gaps to prevent them from being taken by surprise, particularly at night or when there is fog. When the positions become definitive, the gaps between groups have to be set up in a way that makes them continuous riflemen positions.

dows and fields. The captain, followed by the company drummer and bugler, orders them into platoon formation and straight away afterwards the platoon leader's command rings out: « *First section, dispersed formation by the left, at five steps interval. Go.* » Almost like on exercise, the platoon leader takes up position just slightly forward and to the middle of his men, with the two men in charge of calculating the distances, a little behind the NCOs, then the line of riflemen.

As soon as they begin advancing, the dull sound of artillery increases and becomes progressively louder. In front of Michael, on a slight crest, is a village, no doubt the objective to be taken. The enemy is not yet visible. No sooner does the company advance than they come under fire from the infantry facing them. Later on, prisoners tell them that the white or greyish parts of the upturned sleeves and open collars made good targets. An order is given by the company commander: « *Take up your positions. Begin advancing by platoons and, after the fourth jump forward, advance by squads! With God for the Emperor and the Fatherland!* »

Now, Michael hears more and more the shriek of the shells that pass through the air, the shouts and the crack of bullets; at each leap forward, the hail of projectiles becomes clearly heavier. The comrade to the right of Michael suddenly stops and keels over; at the next moment, it's the man on the left who falls over when running. However, the attack continues, with each forward movement, Michael's squad leader shouts: « *One leap forward. Go!* » At the end of each spurt, the men throw themselves heavily onto the ground. The movements are carried out when the German machine guns fire.

Breathless, Michael advances following the orders, and still there is no cover. In front of the platoon is some scrub, then a small stream, and beyond a bank. The men throw themselves forward, catch their breath, then finally the enemy can be seen. An order is barked out: « *Set your sights at 600. Fire at will!* ».

Now, the company can energetically return the enemy fire. The enemy is visible, organised into lines of riflemen, kneeling down behind piles of wheat. The red trousers stand out against the surroundings. Michael sees in front new waves of riflemen arriving, spread out and running,

with the skirts of their greatcoats flapping on both sides. The French artillery still barks out; it is lucky that the shells are going over the heads of the attackers. The German artillery joins in, violent and apparently effective; it supports its infantry as they move forward.

By advancing further, Michael and his platoon pass by an abandoned enemy position near the road leading to the village. For some unknown reason, the order to pursue does not come. « *Take up the prone firing position!* ». The men remain flat on the ground for a while, and Michael sees that the entrance to the village is being attacked by another unit. Then, the company advances. The main road is a terrible sight, covered with the corpses of men and horses, equipment, rifles and so on. French prisoners are lined up against a wall, guarded by a few soldiers. Michael's company is gathered together at one of the corners of the square in front of the church. The squads form up as usual, but there are obvious gaps. Roll call is carried out by platoon. Michael notes with sorrow that neither his « locker comrade », nor his room mate answer the call. The roll call over, the company goes back along the road by which it came.

Word goes round the ranks, although no corresponding order has been heard by the leaders, that they have to go and find the packs. During the attack under enemy fire, the order was given to leave them. Michael was rather happy to do this, every time he threw himself to the ground, the right hook of his backpack strap, which fixed onto the loop at the rear of the ammunition pouch, came off. He had to struggle to fix it before the next advance, otherwise his pack would weigh too much to the rear, and his belt, weighed down by the two ammunition pouches, would pull heavily on one side, making all the equipment unbalanced. When the order got to him, he left his pack behind a tree, and he put the bread bag strap around his neck, fixing the two clips to the ammunition pouch loops, thus making a temporary, but practical and regulation suspension strap.

Michael easily finds his pack. On the road back with his comrades, some of the dead have already been gathered, no doubt to be taken to a burial site. French packs that are found are searched, whatever seems to be of interest such as clean clothing, chocolate, bread, and other foods and various objects are taken.

In the evening, some of the regiment is assembled on three sides near the village cemetery. Nearby, graves have been dug. On the free side, is the regimental band and the three regimental flags (one per battalion). The colonel stands in front. He gives a brief farewell speech, the band plays « *I had a comrade* », a designated group advances towards the graves and fires a salvo. After, the companies file out one after the other and march up the main road.

The beginning of Ersatz

There were three things: wartime intelligence, economic conditions and the formation of regiments made up of volunteers and not part of the mobilisation plans, that lead to the modification of uniforms and equipment. This led to the hasty and intensive manufacture of items with replacement materials (Ersatz). The autumn of 1914 saw the arrival of helmets whose metallic parts were in coppered iron or any other light coppered metal in place of brass.

Some very early models are found in iron, identical to the model 1895, the crown, neck guard and front visor were in black varnished tin instead of varnished black leather. As recruits were incorporated, they were issued more and more with helmets where the leather was replaced by Ersatz materials other than tin: felt, cork, boiled cardboard covered with cloth etc. Items looking vaguely like military helmets were also requisitioned from the police and fire services. On these ad hoc helmets, a cover identical to the model 1892, helps maintain the illusion.

From Autumn 1914 also, given the huge needs and economic restraints, haversacks were more or less made along the lines of the regulation model 1895, initially in strong canvas and cow skin, with a fur flap. They differed by varyingly important modifications and the materials used. Generally, they were made from the strong waterproof grey canvas.

AUTUMN 1914.
MICHAEL
DIGS IN

On October 15, the regiment leaves the billets and heads for the lines. During the march to the lines, Michael hears two officers talking. The regiment is going to take up position between two others, in an area that has yet to be organised; the fourth regiment of the division will remain in reserve. Without any help from the pioneers, the arriving unit will have to organise a coherent trench system; this will entail digging them, then adding the finishing touches whilst possibly being exposed to enemy

fire. Security measures will, therefore, be taken, even though there is no sign of the enemy opposite.

The company commander leads his men to an area that he demarcates with his three platoon leaders. In the distance, Michael sees him tracing out the ground that, in a few hours, will be a trench.

Next, accompanied by the staff, officers and NCOs, he decides where the positions of platoons, flanking systems, the emplacement of shelters and other important details. As soon as a platoon knows its position, the men stand side by side on the indicated line, at a distance of an outstretched arm.

From his position, up to the man on his right, each man makes a narrow scrape which determines the inside edge of the dig. When digging, they go as fast as possible, so that the depth needed to fire from a standing position can be reached. The dug up soil is placed to one side and will be used later for the parapet. It is only when each soldier can fire from the standing position that the hole is enlarged towards that on the right. It gradually dawns on Michael that the company position will not be a straight line. Adapted to the topography, it will be made up of several irregular and angular linking portions. He also notices that the trench does not run directly along the forward slope facing the enemy but is slightly to the reverse of the crest, although it leaves a field of fire of at least 200 metres. The work is hard with the entrenching tools. Luckily a motor car arrives with requisitioned tools, those of the regimental truck are no doubt not enough.

They remain in the sector for ten days, with French patrols occasionally causing problems, opening fire before being chased off by the artillery. Work on the trenches

does not stop ; after digging the fire trench, they have to make observation posts on the crest of the hill, communication trenches plus shelters and so on. The regiment regularly sends patrols out, notably at night. This is to – among others – give cover to the men working on setting up a wooden pickets and barbed wire network. In some places, this network is 15 to 20 metres wide. When the regiment is relieved, the work is not finished. The task will no doubt be continued by the unit that takes over the lines.

On October 26, the regiment is relieved and arrives in a village at the same time as a column of ambulances. They transport twenty stretcher cases, wounded by a French bombardment that caught a working party by surprise. They are taken to a field hospital set up in a village post office equipped with two operating theatres and a reception room. They are hospitalised in the village school. The church, with its red cross flag, is used to treat less serious cases and men who have fallen ill. At the nearby washing place, requisitioned French women wash clothing, sheets and bandages.

In the evening, shells fall on the village. One of them hits the church near the chancel. Stretcher bearers and other medical personnel are wounded. Five wounded men are killed and 17 wounded again. The rest of the medical personnel and the wounded are immediately removed to part of the village that is more sheltered due to the topography. Out of spite or vengeance, the population is gathered together in the church. Companies are assigned to roundup civilians, Michael's company is chosen to guard the church the first night and the following day. It is an unenviable task to guard the elderly, women and children who have nothing and who are frightened. Later

In a plain where the French and Germans fought in August 1914, two officers have been hastily buried. Several months after, even though the grave has been slightly decorated, it remains virtually as it was. (Musées de la Cour d'Or, Metz)

At the edge of a village, the mass grave of men who fell in the first fighting. During the war, it was ringed and a monument was erected in its centre. (J-C. Laparra Collection)

French civilians temporarily locked up in a church and guarded by soldiers. (J-C. Laparra Collection)

In a village that sometimes comes under shell fire, bunk beds have been installed in a cellar. (2007) (M. Tulfournier Collection)

they have to take them one by one to a nearby ruined building so they can relieve themselves. They then have to listen to them complaining of the cold, thirst and hunger. Michael learns later that this ordeal lasted for ten days and that some people with illnesses and young children did not survive.

Generally speaking, rest periods in villages behind the front lines are not very pleasant. These grey houses of these towns and villages bear the scars of war on their facades and roofs. Wary and ragged civilians are rarely seen; the women avoid the soldiers. Only the children, with their curiosity, approach the soldiers, notably the field kitchens, taking whatever is doled out to them.

One of these rest periods is interrupted by a work party. The barbed wire in front of the trenches has to be reinforced on divisional orders. The necessary materiel is stocked in an engineer's dump. It is taken up to the second line positions by the supply column. Then, Michael's battalion has to carry it up to the front lines on their backs. The wire is placed by the units holding the positions.

Michael is happy to avoid this unpleasant and quite dangerous part of the job that is carried out within range of the enemy rifles and machine guns. Kneeling down or standing up in the night, they have to drive stakes into the ground at regular intervals whilst trying

In a village a few kilometres behind the front lines, the soldiers are billeted in buildings that can still be used. In the daytime, tasks are carried out in the street, barns or ground floors of houses.
The cellars are used for sleeping, as they are safer than the ground floor in the case of a night bombardment. They are equipped with roughly made bunks. (Musées de la Cour d'Or, Metz)

A telephone exchange installed in a cellar. (J-C. Laparra Collection)

In a village behind the lines

The German army occupied empty houses, partly or totally requisitioned or those whose occupants had been forced out. When relatively close to the front lines, even cellars were used.

to muffle the sound (the screw pickets will be delivered in a few months time). Two men carry the spool of wire on a stake and others wind it around the stakes. In the darkness it is very difficult to carry out these tasks as the long barbs of the wire rip clothing and hands especially.

Later, Michael is part of a liaison group that has to go to a village that houses the divisional staff. Upon arriving in the main square they see much going on; the quartermasters of all units are there with their wagons. Bread is piled high and tins of food clatter together. Bails of straw are piled on top of each other. The quartermaster personnel walk about with long lists. They talk with supply NCOs about the amount of rations. Marmalade is taken from huge barrels and weighed. Men greet each other as they see each other here every morning. Post is distributed; the army postal service is something that works well! Sacks of mail, full of parcels, letters and cards are flung one after the other onto wagons.

In his notebook, at the date of 11 December 1914, Michael has written. « *First issue of hand grenades* ». These are no doubt round shaped grenades and Michael and his comrades learn how to use them, probably on a voluntary basis. The instructors are pioneers who have come especially to supervise this training.

During this time, and making the most of a period behind the lines, some men are sent to the divisional engineer workshops, where they make racket grenades under the supervision of the pioneers. These stopgap grenades are made from regulation explosive blocks attached to a wooden handle. A simple phosphorous fuse or a slow burning fuse is used to set it off. Michael thus manages to get a glimpse of the workshops and what they are all about. The workshop is set up in and around a large farm

Screw pickets

These were used to make barbed wire defences noiselessly and rapidly in the immediate vicinity of the enemy as well as for repairing existing wire defences that were made either with wooden stakes or partly destroyed. Their coiled end allowed them to be screwed into the ground by turning them with the aid of sticks placed through the loops. In this way, the pickets could be turned whilst in the prone position.

(Information gathered from the war relative to field fortifications. June 1915. German document translated by the S.T.G., 1915.)

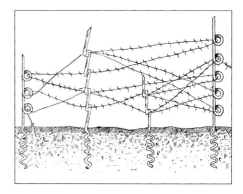

a long way from the village. Nobody smokes here, as it does not only serve as a dump for tools, barbed wire, pickets, planks, beams and sand bags etc. Michael sees piles of wicker carriers that are in fact used to transport minenwerfer projectiles, as well as crates of signal flares and so on. He has also learnt that blocks of dynamite are stored in one of the farm's cellars, with another used for storing the detonators. Working here has also allowed Michael to see that the workshops are used to make all sorts of stopgap measure grenades.

December 15 sees the arrival of items destined to improve the winter issue. Michael is given a second blanket. Also, thanks to the gifts of the Volunteer Medical Assistance Corps (Freiwillige Krankenpflege), he receives a cap comforter that covers the ears, a scarf and a pair of woollen arm warmers. For the sentries, there are also a few rare pairs of felt boots or shoes, allocated in each unit.

A few days later, upon opening a letter with his father's writing on the envelope, he has a painful surprise. The letter contains a wartime card notifying a death. The card bears the photo of his brother in uniform, his name, unit and date and place of his death as well as a prayer. The other side bears a religious illustration. The letter enclosed with the card says that his brother, a wartime volunteer, was part of a reserve regiment that belonged to one of the student divisions part of the 4th Army, and that he died in November near

The first grenades

The first hand grenade to be used was a close quarter combat weapon, initially designed for fighting in fortresses. This was the round model 1913 Kugelhandgranate, 80 mm in diameter and weighing 825 grams of which 117 were the explosives.

It was particularly used for defence against attacks. It had to be thrown from a shelter or into an enemy trench, as the splinters could hit the thrower and the men around him even if far away.

It could be thrown by hand up to approximately 30 metres and up to 300 metres with a catapult. The splinters could go through a pine plank up to a distance of 10 metres. One essential condition for these grenades to remain usable was to store them somewhere dry. Faced with the growing need for grenades, a more easily manufactured model, as it had less fragmentary sections, was designed; this was the model 1915 grenade.

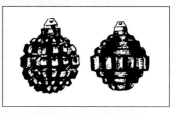

Model 1913 and 1915 grenades. (Hesse Coll.)

Wartime volunteers (Kriegsfreiw.) standing around a NCO The considerable amount of volunteers allowed for the formation of a fourth army corps within the 4th Army. Because of the high proportion of high school pupils, apprentices, students and teachers with these volunteers, the German military cemetery of Langemarck-Nord was called the students' cemetery. (J-C. Laparra Collection)

An infantryman's death notice. The soldier has « died a hero's death for his country ». The illustration shows the Virgin Mary appearing in front of the dying soldier and saying : « I wish to console you with the tender love of a mother ». (J-C. Laparra Collection)

Langemarck during the battle that is known as the « massacre of the innocents ».

The official date of his death is the 10th, the day when, in this sector, there were the most deaths (2,000 according to rumour). At the same time, Michael learns that his other brother, a little over 16 years of age, has signed up for preparatory military training (Jugendwehr). His father, torn between pride and worry tells Michael everything. Organised from September in his town with the support of the local authorities and the veterans association, the Jugendwehr is led by reserve officers and NCOs who are too old for mobilisation. It was his brother's boss, who, encouraged by the authorities, convinced him to sign up. They meet up two evening a week and on Sunday afternoons.

Training camps have also been planned as well as visits to monuments. In particular, a trip has to be organised for the patriotic ceremony in front of a huge Germania statue, maybe the Niederwald monument that was erected to commemorate the re-establishment of the empire in 1871. The Jugendwehr program includes drill, using a rifle, shooting, grenade throwing, constructing trenches as well as singing and commenting on war bulletins.

The army postal service (Feldpost)

Mailbags on a train station platform. (P. Hesse Collection)

The interior of a hut that houses a sorting office.
(J-C. Laparra Collection)

Army postmen
fetching the mail
from the Feldpost
offices set up in a
German army
requisitioned French
post office.
(J-C. Laparra
Collection)

The whole of December is exceptionally rainy. Suddenly on the 24th, the weather changes in a few hours. In the evening, everyone suffers from the cold, it is frosty and snow falls. Little by little, the dull, gloomy countryside is covered by snow and offers a traditional image. The countryside looks like what will be later shown on many cards made for the following Christmases.

From 18.00 hrs when the night falls, all movement ceases and silence reigns. Only the dark mass of the sentries, huddled behind the parapet, show that they are still at war. Sporadic rifle shots are heard. In the deep dugout where Michael is, stands a small Christmas tree ; it is lit up by pieces of burning candle. Most of the men sleep or slumber. Around midnight, some of them begin singing a Schumann *Lied*, then « *Watch on the Rhine* », and calm returns. The following morning, the divisional chaplain, accompanied by the commander of the regiment, that of the battalion and also the company, goes around the positions and talks to each man. The chaplain is the one that Michael saw at the beginning of the campaign. With the group of visitors gone, some say that he should be saluted like an officer and that he is very attached to it.

A young volunteer of the military preparation.
As no official uniform had been decided in order to take part in the activities, his parents have bought his clothes and equipment, thus giving him a vague military appearance.
Only the arm band shows that he is a member of the Jugendwehr.
(P. Hesse Collection)

Christmas 1914. The sector is quiet and, in the support lines, it is possible to gather in front of a dugout.
(P. Hesse Collection)

An NCO with a scope mounted hunting carbine of civilian origin. (L'Illustration No 3781, August 21, 1915).

that it fires the model 1888 cartridge and that it seems more fragile than the regulation model 1898 rifle.

On the 20th, at the billets, the morning parade is told that a uniform modification is to be made by a decree of the 9th of the same month. The shoulder straps have to be sewn onto the tunics. Michael therefore sews on his only available pair onto his tunic; in the day extra pairs, hastily made and without piping, are issued, they go onto the greatcoats.

Return to the trenches. During the night of the 26th to the 27th, there is an alert, the order is given to leave the dugouts. The sentries remain at their posts, especially the combat positions. Behind, in the support trenches, where there are deeper dugouts, all men of rank and those not on duty are lined up. Michael learns that it is to celebrate the emperor Wilhelm II's birthday, and at the same time to disturb the French.

At midnight, a triple « hurra ! » goes up, then each man returns to his dugout to get some sleep.

On February 1, Michael is part of a night time fatigue party bringing up rifle grenades. Starting from the advance engineers dump set up in a ruined hamlet, they have to bring up the ammunition into the front line support trench. Issued at the same time are the racks needed to carry out launching. The fatigue party strings out into a long line, due to the safety gaps between carriers. In places where men can get lost, men are placed to point them in the right direction. Upon returning from the task, men are chosen for launching the grenades and receive theoretical and practical instruction from the pioneers who have come especially for this. However, to avoid stirring up the enemy, no grenade is launched in his direction.

On March 9, towards the end of a rest period at the rear, Michael's regiment swaps its model 1898 Mausers for captured Russian rifles. Michael's rifle is taken away, that he had, necessarily, looked after perfectly. He is issued with a rifle that still has mud in the bolt. A joke does the rounds ; the rifles were recovered a few days ago in the final phase of the fighting in the Masurian region.

Cases of cholera and typhus increased from the autumn of 1914. However, there is no mention of vaccinations in Michael's notebooks before the month of March 1915. On the 18th, with the regiment in the rear, Michael is given a first injection. The liquid is injected under the skin. The stretcher bearers warn the vaccinated men that they will have a high temperature in the evening. Michael does not feel well. During the night, he is chased by all sorts of violent images. When he wakes up, it is light. The straw inside of his mattress crackles. A man nearby groans. Michael gets up and realises that it is sore where he had the injection. The call to get up will not be long and normal duties will resume. A second injection is carried out on the 24th, whilst the regiment is ready to move back up to the front lines. A booster will be carried out in roughly one month, according to circumstances.

Another rest period. One morning in mid April, it is announced that the band of the round cap is too visible (it is red for the infantry) and that it will be covered by a removable strip of grey canvas, on the orders of the

A propaganda postcard used for sending season's greetings. Autumn 1914 - Spring 1915. The alliance between the Germans and the Austrians was at its height. It was celebrated on various items : postcards, glasses, plates, drinks labels and so on.
Here is a Feldpostkarte sent on January 12, 1915, to someone living in Rhénanie-Palatinat, bearing the inscription :
« We will hold on together, firm and loyal ».
(J-C. Laparra Collection)

The day is cold but without snow or rain, and is relatively peaceful. The artillery in particular slumbers. On the 26th, it is back to reality and the guns wake up on both sides. On the 27th, bad weather returns with heavy snowfall. The 28th sees a strong thunderstorm, as If the gods wished to signal a real return to hostilities. The trenches fill with water, some of the dugouts have to be pumped out and the ways, that have become unusable, are scraped clear. The sentries, with their feet in the mud, and the men bringing up the soup, suffer particular discomfort. The bad weather continues in this way until the end of the year.

1915.
THE WAR WEARS ON

On January 4, Michael writes down that he has learnt of the issuing of a few hunting carbines with scopes in the regiment. They are given to men of rank or soldiers, chosen from those who wear the marksman's lanyard, on the right hand side of the chest, between right shoulder strap and a tunic button. Later in the day, he sees his company commander with the platoon commanders trying out one of the carbines. One of the officers' batmen, having had the opportunity of seeing one of these weapons close up, tells Michael that it was requisitioned in Germany and

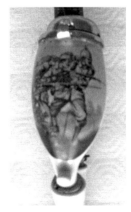

A pipe decorated with a propaganda motif.
(J-C. Laparra Collection)

Static warfare

A communication trench being finished off in a frontline position.
(Der Weltkrieg in seiner Rauhen Wirklichkeit,1926)

After hearing a suspicious noise, the sentry on the left checks his weapon. Two alert NCOs or officers look out over the land in front of the trench. Further away, a man puts his rifle to his shoulder. (J-C. Laparra Collection)

A trench after an enemy direct hit.
(Der Weltkrieg in seiner Rauhen Wirklichkeit, 1926)

Imperial Cabinet dated 29 March 1915. The *Unteroffizier* go to the company quartermaster to get these covers. At the same time, the *Unteroffizier* are issued with a mask to cover their mouth and nose as well as a small phial, to hand out to their men.

At the same time, word gets around that a new way of inflicting losses on the enemy is going to be used by the German army, the release of gas from canisters. All of the combat units are to be equipped with this rudimentary protection. At the Front, it will be attached to the front of the tunic. In the case of the enemy also using it, the soldier will be able to use the cloth mask and its accom-

Rifle grenades

When war broke out, the Germans had limited numbers of the model 1913 rod mounted rifle grenade, with an iron steeled cylinder weighing 900 grams of which 80 were explosives. Designed for use by pioneers in fortress warfare, it was used from the autumn of 1914 in static warfare. Groups of troops, work detachments in forward saps, assault columns and assault material all made excellent targets.

The rifle grenade was usually launched with the rifle fixed to a rack. Launching these grenades without the rack was possible in exceptional circumstances if needed. In such cases, the rifle butt was placed on the ground to absorb the recoil, with a sand bag folded under the butt plate.

The model 1913 grenade was replaced by the improved model 1914. The first rack was the model 1913, another model (1915) was equipped with a system designed to absorb the recoil from the discharged grenade.

Launching a model 1913 rifle grenade, equipped with a range reducing disk. The rifle is mounted on a model 1913 rack. (P. Hesse Collection)

« Our house in the earth »
The name given by a
Landwehr *infantryman to
his dugout in March 1915.
The dugout, no doubt, is in
a support trench in sector
where the trenches are well
made.*
(J-C. Laparra Collection)

A German infantryman
wearing the feldgrau
uniform and equipped with
Model 1895 ammunition
pouches. The leather
equipment has already
been blackened. The rifle is
a Model 1891 Mosin-Nagant
with its original bayonet.
(Mémorial de Verdun,
Fleury-devant-Douaumont)

panying phial. Using the liquid inside the phial, the soldier will impregnate the cloth mask and place it over his mouth using the ties to secure it on his head. The soldiers call it, from the outset of the first training session, the « perfumed pouch ».

On 25 April, in the lines, Michael notes that the machine gun positioned behind his company is now equipped with an armoured cover over the barrel that also protects the lower face of the gunner. On the 29th, whilst carrying out excavation work at the billets, Michael learns that a

The model 1891 rifle

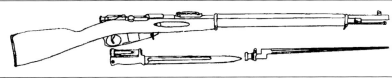

The Russian Model 1891 rifle with two possible types of bayonet, the Russian and the German mounted on the adaptor. (J-C. Laparra Collection)

With a length of 1.288 metres and a weight of 4.200 kg, this rifle is of the Mosin-Nagant system with a magazine carrying five 7.62 cartridges on clips. It was issued in the German army until 1916. The important quantities of weapons (rifles, machine guns, artillery pieces, etc.), munitions and material (carts, field kitchens, etc.), captured from the Russians during the first years of the war, meant that whole units could be equipped.

Generally, it was divisions of new recruits that received Russian weapons, remaining issued with them for a certain time. Regular units also received model 1891 rifles, for example the 39th Fusilier Regiment and the 76th Infantry Regiment. The rifle was also often used for training and for equipping Landsturm units or billet town services. Later, some of these rifles were adapted for firing German 7.92 mm ammunition.

This rifle's bayonet was 0.445 metres in length and weighed 0.200 kg. As the Russian infantry kept it permanently fixed to the rifle, it did not come with a scabbard.

The German arsenals made one in grey painted tin, so that this bayonet could be worn on the belt. It was also possible to fix standard German bayonets to this Russian rifle thanks to a cylindrical cover.

The German arsenals also made two models with ferrule especially for captured rifles.

*Vaccinations against typhus
or cholera. This is carried
out in a camp behind the
front lines in front of a
company aid post.
(Musées de la Cour d'Or,
Metz)*

tools wagon has been issued to each battalion. Up to now, there had only been one per regiment.

On 25 May, a word from the regimental commander states that it is forbidden to noticeably wear private purchase daggers. The only ones to be authorised are those that are going to be issued according to a war ministry notification dating from the 8th of this month. This brings an end to a trend that had started to spread.

On 5 June, the regiment gets to change its Russian rifles for German model 1888/1905 rifles.

In July, Michael's regiment spends most of the month on earthwork detail. They are reinforcing a second posi-

*Close up of a vaccination.
Throughout the war, the
German high command
paid special attention to
the prevention of disease.
The prevention of
epidemics was important,
notably against typhus.
Campaigns of vaccination
began in mid November
1914.
(Mémorial de Verdun,
Fleury-devant-Douaumont)*

The consequences of war

Following a measure taken on April 6, 1915, to economise copper and brass, uniforms no longer had buttons or hooks made from these metals. Even the brass belt buckles were to be replaced by an iron equivalent painted in grey.

As well as this, from now on, the leather items such as belts, ammunition pouches, backpack straps, boots and so on, were blackened. Personal equipment, water bottle, mess tin and cup were no longer made of iron but of aluminium.

The bayonet saw its scabbard replaced by a tin equivalent and was shortened, those issued from 1915/1916 were most often entirely made from metal and roughly machined.

tion that is three to six kilometres behind the front line trenches. This position comprises of a trench barbed wire in front, whilst the front line trenches comprise three to five lines of trenches or positions, protected by barbed wire and covered by strong points made up of dugouts or concrete blockhouses. The French heavy artillery has tried to disrupt the work but with no success. This second line is virtually out of sight of the enemy observers, because of the topography. Added to this, the French no doubt do not have enough artillery pieces and have an inadequate supply of munitions. Above all, much of the work is carried out at night. The result is that at the end of this month all of the men are tired.

Real rest is given for a few days. The heavy July nights weigh heavily on the company billets and on the sleep of 150 men harassed by the exhausting work. The men

The Bavarian dagger that saves lives

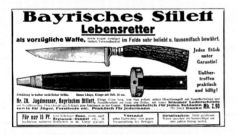

A newspaper advert for a dagger « a must have for every soldier ». It could save lives or be used for other uses when on campaign.
(Deutsche Kriegszeitung N° 30 25.Juli 1915)

sleep on three tier bunks with steel bases (in fact chicken wire stretched over a wooden frame) and mattresses filled with wood shavings (straw and hay is now kept for horses), where they turn, groan and scratch without waking up. The company is infested with lice. It had come away clean and as if regenerated from the huge delousing establishment, where it had been a few weeks previously. The stay in the second line during almost a month has left its mark, despite the use, on an individual basis, of various

anti louse products. As well as this, being in the present billet has led to the current infestation. Before settling down in the dirty, rat inhabited billets, the battalion clears up the mess left around the buildings by the previous occupants. However, the yellowish lice, hidden in the stit-

The model 1888 rifle

A recruit posing for the photographer after being issued with his « funeral clothes ». He has a model 1888 rifle or one of the modified models. The bayonet is of a simplified Ersatz type which leads us to assume that the photo is no doubt after 1915. (J-C. Laparra Collection)

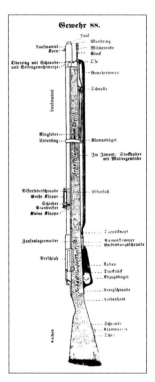

The model 1888 rifle.
(Dilthey's militärischer Dienst-Unterricht für Einjährig-Freiwillige, 1906)

This weapon was designed by the Imperial Control Commission for rifles and reunited both the Mauser and Mannlicher systems. It was the first model of the German army whose design integrated an outer magazine and a small calibre cartridge (7.92mm) using a low smoke powder.

This rifle, 1.245 m long, was lighter than the model 1898 (3.800 kg). It was transformed with the creation of the S ammunition and was designated as the model 1888 S. It then became the models 1888/1905 and 1888/1914 when it was modified to take ammunition clips like on the model 1898 rifle and the model 1898a carbine.

The bayonet initially destined for the model 1888 rifle was the model 1871.

The rifle could also be equipped with the models 1865/71, 1871/84 (Jäger) and the 1871/84 (short model). During the war it used captured and Ersatz bayonets.

An example of a private purchase anti louse product bought whilst on leave or sent by families.
(J-C. Laparra Collection)

Life behind the front lines.
An abattoir supplying meat for an army corps.
(P. Hesse Collection)

In billets, a regimental workshop for making cold meats.
(J-C. Laparra Collection)

ching of the bags of the same colour, have patiently awaited their hour and now it is here! As a « philosopher » says to Michael who is complaining, « *Lice are like officers and fate: superior creatures with whom you have to be on your guard, while at the same time having to pretty well put up with them.* »

On 15 August, Michael notes that from today, all the officers and senior NCOs are issued, without exception and even at the rear, with a short bayonet in place of the sabre.

Towards the beginning of October, the regiment is at rest, the weather is good. Men are often sent to help the supply troops cut and collect grass in a field. Even though he does not really know how to use a scythe, Michael has volunteered in order to get some exercise and escape from any possibly more disagreeable chores. At the other side of the stream, he sees the divisional veterinary hospital (*Pferdelazarett*) setting up. Under a tent, skeletal, exhausted artillery horses are attended to.

A little further on, requisitioned French villagers and a few Russian prisoners work in a field, guarded by German soldiers. Towards evening time, the quartermasters organise the issuing of protective goggles and the exchange of anti gas mouth pads for improved models.

There is an incident during the period at the rear. The squad to which Michael belongs is now commanded by a new *Unteroffizier* who has come up from the depot. He is older than his subordinates and does not get on with them. A postman in civilian life, he has, according to some, the rigid sense of duty that characterises the Prussians. A disagreement degenerates into confrontation between the *Unteroffizier* and two soldiers over the application of an order. The order, dated 21 September 1915 from the Imperial cabinet, defines a new campaign uniform with all the issue personal leather items having to be blackened with dye or black polish, boots, belt, backpack straps and so on. This is in fact a renewal of the measure of the previous 6 April. The conditions for

Michael's squad carrying out this order are such that two men protest. The *Unteroffizier* goes and complains to the company adjutant. In the evening, after roll call, there is a confrontation. In the company office, the lieutenant who has taken over from the captain sits and calls everybody in, one after the other. Michael is called as a witness and explains why some of his comrades have rebelled. The *Unteroffizier* is called in and Michael repeats what he has said. *« Is this true? »* the lieutenant asks the *Unteroffizier*. The latter is ill at ease and ends up by admitting that Michael is right. The lieutenant rebukes him and saying that the Front is not the parade ground and that one needs to have a way of commanding adapted to the situation and that he will be transferred to another platoon. He then calls in the two soldiers that protested, they both receive a rollicking, one ends up with three days in the guardroom, with the other getting one day. Prison has been avoided, the sentence would have been carried out in a cellar or a small and guarded room. As for the punishment of being tied to a tree for several hours, at this stage of the war, it is no longer carried out.

Explaining to the two men, that despite the NCO being in the wrong, sacrosanct discipline must be saved; the officer adds that it is impossible to act in any other way. The company adjutant, therefore, leads the two men to the guardhouse, in fact an old chicken house. It will be possible for discreet visitors to sneak up to it. One hour after the two men are locked in behind the wire, Michael and some of his comrades come up to them and give them a little chocolate and some cigarettes. Then everyone plays scat into the night.

On 14 December, before going back to the front lines, gas masks are issued. This new piece of equipment comprises of the mask proper, covering the face, and a changeable *feldgrau* painted filter that screws onto the mask, containing neutralising substances. Near each eye piece, there is a small pocket, at eye level, upon which is glued, on the inside, a rectangular piece of felt that can be used to wipe away condensation without removing the mask.

The gas mask

The first model rubberised canvas gas mask.
(Private Collection)

Soldiers near the Front line. They wear the mask in the
alert position. (J-C. Laparra Collection)

This piece of equipment was first noted at the Front in September 1915. It was not fully issued until March 1916. It was made from a cloth covered with a thin layer of rubber (from which its usual name of Gummimaske, and the rarer Zeppelin, comes from).

It had two parallel elastic cloth straps, sewn onto each side of the mask, that kept it attached to the face. This was modified with the addition of a central Y strap that improved the way the mask was held in place. Towards the month of March, another type appeared, also in rubberised cloth. The layer of rubber was thicker, also, the amplitude of the mask, enough to allow the felt to be moved with the index finger and wipe the condensation off the eye pieces, was reduced, which improved the breathing via the filter, but it was not a perfect seal.

The straps were also modified again in June 1916.

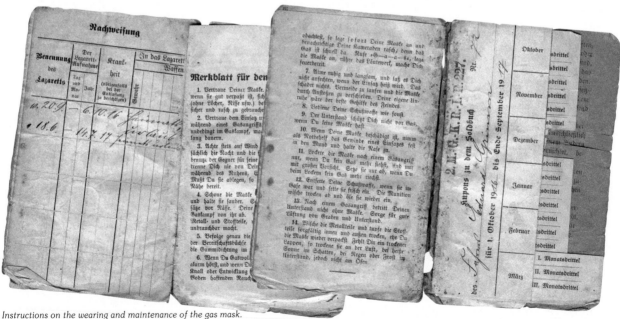

Instructions on the wearing and maintenance of the gas mask.
These were stuck into the Soldbuch. (R. Kopp. Collection)

A scene characteristic of the summer of 1915. The men still have their improved anti gas mouth pads and wear the small carrying pouch on their chest. They have already been issued with model 1915 stick grenades (one is hung on the belt of the NCOs in the middle ground in the trench). Note that they still have racket grenades. (Musées de la Cour d'Or, Metz)

The issuing of the masks is also the moment to test their seal and also the chance to laugh a little. The assembled company forms a column and has to file down a covered trench in which bottles of a type of tear gas have been broken, producing a light cloud of gas. Woe betide the

man who has not put his mask on properly, he leaves the trench coughing and with eyes streaming to the mirth of his comrades. The pay books are collected together and taken to the company office, instructions on looking after the mask, in the form of a leaflet, are stuck inside each pay book. The size of the mask is also written down according to a list made up by squads.

For Christmas, making the most of the relief of the regiment and its stay in billets in the rear, the regiment inaugurates the new leather helmets with a removable spike. They are issued by regiment. The new black varnished leather helmet is almost identical to the previous model. Michael is also issued with a two part helmet cover (one for the helmet and one for the spike) made from a greenish grey cloth. The quartermasters tell the men that felt numbers for sewing onto the cover, will not be issued. On Christmas day, gifts are handed out *(Liebesgaben)* sent by the Red Cross *(Freiwillige Krankenpflege)* and wartime soldiers' welfare funds, these include tins of cigarettes, cigars and brandy, other items to celebrate the occasion in a fitting way and warm clothing.

Christmas at the Front. « Silent night, Holy night ». This corresponds to the famous Christmas carol and to the beginning of each verse. This carol, of Austrian origin, was composed in 1816 and put to music in 1818. This card was sent on 20 December 1915 by an infantryman stationed at Osnabrück to his parents in Obernai. It shows three artillery men with their ball topped helmets, on the alert near a Model 1910 210 mm mortar.
(J-C. Laparra Collection)

The new spiked helmet

A new helmet was worn with the uniform made official on 21 September 1915. It had a removable spike that screwed onto the base with a bayonet fitting, that was no longer worn at the Front. All the iron fittings were painted grey.

In many series, the leather used to make the helmet was replaced by Ersatz (generally felt or tin). The campaign helmet cover was maintained, but in two parts.

On some Ersatz models, the helmet and fittings were painted in feldgrau or khaki which allowed the cover to be dispensed with.

On this one, the unit number disappeared after the order of 27 October 1916.

A model 1915 Prussian spiked helmet. The same helmet with its cover. (J-C. Laparra Collection)

A few examples of an infantryman's personal items. From top to bottom and left to right. Identity tags (three model 1878, one model 1915 and a model 1916). Items bought from the canteen, (a small glass with a propaganda motif that contained fruit in alcohol, a cup with a propaganda motif, cigarettes, a holder for a small box of matches), German coins, a metal holder for three cigars, a box of cigars of the « Armed heroes » brand (Waffenheld), whose tricolour band says that they are given to « German NCOs » (there were ordinary models for privates). On both sides two earthenware brandy bottles (Steinhager) by the firm « H.W. Schlichte, the oldest Steinhagen distillery ». (J-C. Laparra Collection)

1916. THE GERMAN ARMY IS WORN DOWN

On 1 January, the armourers change all of the model 1888/05 rifles for the model 1898.

The next relief is in mid January. A group of young men arrive from Germany, sent by the regimental recruit depot. They are shared out amongst the companies, including that of Michael that is billeted in the village church where the battalion is billeted. At this time, the core is still formed of soldiers of the classes of 1912 to 1914. All the companies also have wartime volunteers in their ranks, some of whom were allocated to their units in the autumn. There are another two with the new arrivals. The men get to know each other. One is a Jew, he his the son of a successful shopkeeper, totally integrated and an utter patriot. When war was declared, this young man was only 16 years old and ill. Once better, he joined up due to a sense of duty as many boys of his age did. The other is more outgoing and is mad keen on the war, this type of recruit is known as a *Kriegsmutwillige*, a humorous nickname based on a play on the words *Krieg* (war) and *mutwillig* (willingly), it is used for wartime volunteer *Kriegsfreiwillige*, meaning joined up for the duration of the war. The newly arrived man takes a completely non regulation cap with a varnished leather visor, from his backpack. Michael says to him « *That's your head scratcher isn't it? It wasn't the Prussians that gave you that Sunday best cap. The sergeant will look twice at you when he sees you with that.* »

Michael then helps the new arrivals prepare their lightened packs, known as the « assault pack ». At the recruit depot, the instructors teach the men how to put together

The influence of the war on materiel. Raw materials were increasingly qualified as Ersatz (felt, iron, various mixes of metals, inferior quality tin and so on. (J-C. Laparra Collection)

the lightened pack. This is the rolled up greatcoat, held by straps and passed over the left shoulder and down to the right at waist level, the mess tin hangs on the rolled greatcoat at the back. However, this is an old fashioned way of doing things. At the Front, it is not done in this way, firstly the mess tin has the blanket rolled around it, followed by the tent, all of this held together by backpack straps. This is then held on the soldier thanks to the bread bag strap. Michael also finds a strip of cloth for his « disciples » and shows them how to cover the breeches of their rifles as there is not a purpose made breech cover. One will be made available in the spring of this year but its issue will not be generalised. He also checks to see if the young recruits have sewn the two field dressings into the front skirts of their tunics. Michael has two extra ones that he found and that he has put, as a precaution, in his bread bag. He is also going to test out a pair of straps that his parents have sent him; these are supposed to improve the way the feet sit in the boots, especially when they sink into mud, by holding them tighter at the ankles.

The regiment goes into the line, no doubt in a hot sector, if the precise orders that have been given concerning what has to be taken, are anything to go by. No backpack, the helmet without the spike (model 1915 helmet), the greatcoat to be worn as it is very cold and sleet falls from the leaden sky. They carry, as seen previously, a blanket, tent and mess tin, held by the bread bag strap. There are three or four tinned rations in the bread bag and the water bottle filled with tea hangs from it. Each rifle equipped soldier has 200 rounds of ammunition, held in the pouches, pockets and in the bandoleers slung around the neck and over the chest. Each man has about three grenades, several sandbags that can be filled if needed, portable trench shields, wire cutters and tools.

The requisition of churches by the occupying army

A church used as a billet (postmarked 3 January 1916). (J-C. Laparra Collection)

A church hospital. (P. Hesse Collection)

A church used as stables. (J-C. Laparra Collection)

Churches were sometimes left at the disposition of the French clergy who had to, nonetheless, give priority to the German military chaplains. Churches were often transformed for other uses.

The model 1916 rifle breech cover.
In the centre of the photograph, a man carries his rifle on his back, the breech is protected by a unit issued cover. The photograph portrays the distribution of a meal. Men, with extra model 1913 ammunition bandoleers, hold their mess tins.
(J-C. Laparra Collection)

The boot straps designed to improve the support of the feet in the boots.
This system patented in 1910, was tried out in different army corps but was not generalised. It was attested on an individual basis from 1914 to 1916.
(Kriegstechnische Zeischrift, 1910).

The destination is a sector that covers an old isolated largefarm. Not easily spotted, as it has been demolished by artillery, it is situated in the main line of resistance and has been transformed into a strongpoint. Michael's company has been tasked with improving the position, trenches and communication trenches have to be widened, duckboards made and fitted to the muddy trench floors. Michael's platoon shelters in the cellars of the old farm. When they are not on duty (sentry or work), the men clean their weapons or scrape the mud off their boots, trousers and greatcoats. At the end of sentry duty, tired and with a heavy head, Michael goes back to the cellars where his snoring comrades lay. Although he is used to it, he is hit by the smells within the wet walls. He kneels down in a relatively clean corner that he made earlier by laying some planks side by side that he found, making a floor of at least two square metres. He lights a small stearin trench candle, takes off his tunic that he folds and uses as a pillow, puts on his

greatcoat and settles down, covering his wooden boards with his folded tent section. Finally, he pulls his blanket onto himself ; he has left his other one on his backpack back at the billets. Once settled down, he manages to sleep. He is woken up at dawn by « Franz » (the nickname given to the French) who lays down a heavier than usual barrage on the sector. He thinks of those who left before sunrise to go and fetch the rations. Towards the end of the night, when, from their observation balloons, the French observers cannot yet make out the terrain, the field kitchens try to get up to a few kilometres from the first lines. In this sector it is impossible to set up permanent foiled kitchens in shelters as there are not any deep ravines or gorges that allow such an activity to be hidden from sight. Rather badly sheltered, the cooks quickly distribute hot food, usually a thick bean soup with pieces of meat or peas with fat. The ration parties then bring back the food in large containers. This morning, the rations will be late again or not come at all. It is a pity as the soldier always feels so much better with a meal in his belly, especially if it is still a bit warm.

Towards the end of January, Michael's regiment sees the arrival of a new model 1916 percussion stick grenade, even though a fuse model has been in existence since the previous year. There not being enough time to organise a collective training session, the grenade is presented during a parade. Given its delicate mechanism, this grenade frequently fails to go off.

February 26 sees the arrival of a few reinforcements. They now arrive from the newly created divisional recruit depot. These youngsters are from the class of 1915, called up from September to November of this year. Some have no doubt undergone a shortened basic training. They are not without

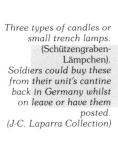

Three types of candles or small trench lamps.
(Schützengraben-Lämpchen).
Soldiers could buy these from their unit's cantine back in Germany whilst on leave or have them posted.
(J-C. Laparra Collection)

Dannevoux.

The field kitchen

The field kitchen, tested from 1908, was developed along with the more commonly used model 1911. It was designed for use with 125 to 250 men, that is a company, squadron or a battery. It underwent modifications in 1913. There was a smaller version, for 60 to 125 men, the models 1912 and 1914. Mostly used within regular units at the beginning of the war, these kitchens were progressively generalised.

Kitchens captured from the enemy were generally reused, especially the Russian model. In soldier's slang, the field kitchen was known as the « Marie Rata » or « Goulash gun ».

A captured Russian model field kitchen.
(J-C. Laparra Collection)

Model 1911 German
field kitchen.
(Private Collection)

A model 1911 field kitchen seen from
above. (P. Hesse Collection)

interest. They have brought with them a new song. They say that many women cried when they heard the song after it had been composed in the last months of the previous year, at the Gürzenich of Cologne, a fashionable concert hall that has remained open during the war. Michael's comrades take it up straight away.

« In the billets when on campaign,
I hear my tired feet on the hard ground
And, at night, I send my darling a thousand kisses.
I have never felt so alone, Anne Marie!

We will still fight bloody battles,
Who knows if I will see you again, darling,
Maybe I will be close to you soon, Anne Marie,
Maybe they will bury me tomorrow, with all the company.

If a bullet hits me I won't come home,
So don't cry, find another man, darling,
Someone young and handsome, Anne Marie.
But not necessarily a man… from my company ».

On May 8, some model 1898 rifles are exchanged in Michael's company for identical models that have undergone the modification to the base of the magazine that will allow the use of removable 25 round magazines. After having handled the new weapons equipped with this new magazine, the men recently issued with them, all good marksmen, find them practical, given the capacity of the magazine, and are fairly happy with them. In the evening, they are all brought together to make up a special unit within one of the platoons.

On June 7, with the regiment at rest in a camp, training sessions on the different types of grenades and how to throw them are organised. The rest period ends with a sports day during which there is a grenade throwing contest. The three best throws are 49, 46 and 44 metres respectively, each man wins two bottles of wine. The average throwing distance for grenades is 30 to 35 metres. During the day, Michael learns of something that is unknown to all, as it has not been mentioned in the despatches. Because of this, it passes from unit to unit, as it is so surprising. On

Fort de Douaumont.
The wall behind which the
dead of the 8 May 1916
remain.
(Schicksalswende am
Douaumont, 1942).

An attack in a sector with no obvious signs of a bombardment
(21 February 1916)

16.02 hrs. An attack from the German lines. A Fielder model 1912 flame thrower team goes through barbed wire entanglements whilst another team must already be in action judging from the smoke on the right. Note in the foreground, an infantryman with a model 1915 spiked helmet (without the spike). The unit on the left, in the background, is ahead of the one being photographed.

16.05 hrs. The attack continues, the fire started by the flame thrower continues to burn. On the left, the neighbouring unit is well ahead.

16.10 hrs. The last men go through the flimsy defences. The fire still burns. On the left, the neighbouring unit is already far ahead.
(1 000 Bilder aus 25 Jahren Deutscher Geschichte)

8 May last, there was a huge explosion in a German held fort near Verdun, it caused the deaths of several hundred men, blown up, burnt and suffocated. In a tunnel, hidden by a few boxes of ammunition, two or three stupid Bavarians wanted to heat up some food in a mess tin, using

Three model 1898 rifles issued to the infantry (1916)
The standard weapon, the rifle with scope, the rifle with the removable magazine

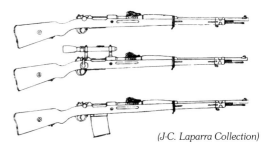

(J-C. Laparra Collection)

Different models of rifles and carbines in service in the German army

(J-C. Laparra Collection)

Model 1898 rifle with breech cover (1917), removable magazine (1916) and model 1898 bayonet.
Model 1898a carbine with model 1898/1905 bayonet.
Model 1898 carbine.
Model 1888 rifle with model 1871 bayonet.
Model 1888 carbine.
Model 1891 carbine.
Model 1908 Mondragon rifle.

powder taken from a hand grenade. When taking the grenade apart, it blew up. Instead of the usual few victims caused by this type of accident, bad luck led to the explosion igniting flame thrower fuel stacked nearby. This spread to very dry pine crates filled with fuses, the flames and explosions then set off hand grenades, and then it was the turn of a dump of shells stacked in a corridor.

July 3, there are now three rifles with scopes in Michael's company, as is the case with the others in the regiment. The marksmen have been chosen on the basis of their results on the ranges, that led to the attribution, before the war, of the marksman's lanyard. Failing this, the best riflemen have been chosen, except for loudmouths and poten-

Two models of grenade used in the summer of 1916. Lenticular shaped percussion model 1915 grenades, known as « toads ». The small model in pre-fragmented iron, weighing 360 grams of which 20 was the explosive), the large model (in tin, weighing 415 grams of which 130 was the explosive). (L'Illustration No 3830 29 July 1916)

tial deserters. Each rifle, a regulation model 1898 with a bent cocking lever, is issued to a marksman who is in charge of its use and maintenance. For any repairs or important adjustments, he has to see the regimental armourer. The marksman is issued with S.K.M. (*Stahlkernmunition*: steel core bullets) rounds for firing against enemy trench shields.

Model 1915 fuse stick grenades with the model 1916 detonating system and base plug. Le modèle le plus largement en usage. (L'Illustration No 3830)

The model 1916 steel helmet

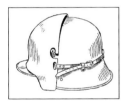

(J-C. Laparra Collection)

The new German helmet with brow plate, according to a French notice of 24 July 1916.

The model 1916 steel helmet (Stahlhelm) made its appearance on 19 February 1916. Well designed but a little heavy (1.175 kg), it gradually replaced the spiked helmet and greatly changed the soldier's appearance. Generalised in 1917 as

The steel helmet with and without the brow plate (April 1916). (M. Sublet Collection)

personal equipment, it underwent modifications during this same year and in 1918, generally keeping its shape. An official note of 7 July 1918, described the way to cover its original *feldgrau* paint with another camouflaged pattern.

This helmet had the particularity of having, on each side, two bolts to which could be attached a steel brow plate of which only 50,000 were made. Made from moulded steel, it weighed 2.080 kg and was held at the rear by a strap. It offered good protection against shell splinters and bullets fired from usual distances, especially British ones.

However, a Lebel bullet, hitting frontally could perhaps penetrate it.

Officers and NCOs with the model 1916 steel helmet. One, in the middle distance, has a cover. (Photograph no doubt dating from 1917). (P. Hesse Collection)

41

Life at the billets :

A bath using the means available.
(J-C. Laparra Collection)

Preparing for rifle inspection.
(J-C. Laparra Collection)

The Zeiss manufactured telescopic sights have a X3 zoom.

The regiment is going back to the trenches on August 15. The company on morning parade is rife with rumour. This was initially started by a few early birds that came back all excited from the huts.

« *Hey boys ! We are definitely going to be given the new steel helmet !* »

It is true that up to now it has not been generalised. Very often it has only been issued to shock troop units within regiments and, during attacks, only the men of the first wave have them. Indeed, during the day, some of the men see, near the *Feldbahn* station (a small 0.60 gauge train), wagons full of these helmets. Later, the adjutant passes by to take head measurements. The helmets are issued during the evening parade and swapped for the leather helmets. Trying them on in the huts is a scene where surprise, rude remarks and jokes are mixed together.

« *Too heavy !* » is the general opinion.

Coming back from the trenches, it is difficult to know what Michael has been through there. He spent three days crouched down in a shell hole where he saw death close up at all times, such as the comrade whose chest was penetrated by a small, sharp shell splinter. Hearing his neighbour suddenly moan, Michael leant over towards him and held up his head. The wounded man opened his tired eyes, wide open with an expression that seemed to be saying, « *It's over !* ». There was no cry of pain, but his body stiffened and his hands gripped. His head, like that of a small girl, lopped to one side. Then his feet and hands beat like the wings of a dying bird. Finally, the movements came to a complete stop. And all this, without the slightest drop of water to drink and in a horrible stench. An exploding shell threw earth over the human remains, the next exposed others. When Michael and his neighbours wanted to dig deeper to gain more shelter, their shovels quickly hit a corpse. Sometimes, at his wits end, a soldier, curled up, began to pray. Later, the relief was also hellish.

Life in the billets is always the same ; the huts have to be cleaned, mud scraped from the paths, potatoes peeled and wood split for the ovens. Rest periods do not really offer proper rest. Units are taken from the companies for fatigues, digging second line positions, moving ammuni-

Roll call for requisitioned labourers in an occupied village (summer 1916) This takes place under the amused gaze of German military personnel. The civilians are going to clean the streets of a town occupied by the German army. At the rear are the young men and some rare menfolk, to the left are the young girls and the female teenagers, to the right the women. These groups were supervised by accompanying personnel or sentries.
(J-C. Laparra Collection)

tion and materiel, guarding prisoners as they make their way to the rear, supervising civilian labourers and so on. Training periods also come one after the other, a reminder of basic training, how to salute superiors, how to come to attention and drill. Some are occasionally more technical, notably grenade throwing. Today, as the afternoon ends with bayonet fencing and the company back at the billets, they thought they were done for the evening. But the *Feldwebel* announces, « *Roll call at 6 o'clock!* » Another inspection to prepare. What is it about this time? This is the fifth time in a few days, for rifles, underwear, twill tunic, field tunic and the neck cloth! This time it is for the pair of ankle boots. « *Company, attention! Fall... out!* » The men disperse calmly under the gaze of the superiors, followed by, a little further on, by recriminations and swearing. How could they, after months of war, continue to treat the soldier like a stupid barrack room recruit? In such conditions, little time remains to clean oneself up, as well as one's kit, wash underclothes and write a few postcards.

To break with the monotony of the trenches, and hoping for better treatment in the future, Michael accepts to be a

Concentrated charge
(Geballte Ladung)

Making a concentrated charge with grenades.
(Anleitung zur Ausbildung von Stosstrupp-Anleitung für Kompanieführer, 1917)

An improvised explosive charge that could be made in the field during an action. It was made up of grenades without their sticks, tied around the body of a grenade which was screwed onto its stick.
The charge was carried and detonated with the stick of the central grenade. It could destroy timbered positions, blow holes in anti grenade meshing in trenches and later, damage tank tracks.

volunteer for a course for shock troops. In this way he hopes to get away from the Front for training periods and benefit, from time to time, from perks such as improved food, the chance to stand out and maybe, therefore, get a medal and even extra leave. He is sent for three weeks on a course organised by the divisional assault company in the village where it is billeted. The company is commanded by two lieutenants, one of whom is a reserve officer, and 12 NCOs.

The course includes the study of trench raids against small positions, surprise attacks, making gaps in barbed wire defences, going through them by crawling or passing over them. They also learn the coordination between the different shock troop groups and the units bringing up materiel and ammunition, and if need be, the following up waves of assault infantry. The course also comprises the infiltration of trenches and communication trenches, the mopping up of enemy positions and reversing the fire step when these are occupied. Training is completed by the making

Some men of an infantry company gather together (May 1916)
In the first two rows, the men of the shock troop (Stosstrupp) with model 1916 steel helmets (the other infantrymen still have the model 1915 spiked helmet with the spike removed), some wear puttees, extra model 1913 ammunition bandoleers around their necks and have model 1898 rifles with cloth breech covers. (J-C. Laparra Collection)

A shock troop group (Stosstrupp), gathered around its leader, an Unteroffizier. In the front row on the right, the Unteroffizier can be identified by the button on the right side of his collar (that on the left side is not visible), he still carries a false knot on his bayonet (which is not a model 1898). The pouch attached to his belt is that of the model 1905 folding cavalry saw, used in the infantry from 1915. Only himself and the man next to him wear puttees; the others have boots. Two men on the left at the front have already won the Iron Cross second class. The model 1898 rifles are worn across the chest and the model 1916 gas masks are worn at the alert. The grenade carrying equipment is fairly basic, the bag straps are not string but strips of sewn cloth. Mémorial de Verdun, Fleury-devant-Douaumont. (Mémorial de Verdun, Fleury-devant-Douaumont)

A demonstration by an officer commanding a shock troop unit in throwing a concentrated charge.
(Kriegskronik des « Daheim » Band 7)

A rather unceremonious soldier's burial in a civilian cemetery requisitioned by the German army. (Musées de la Cour d'Or, Metz)

The aluminium plaque placed on the wooden crosses of German graves. Germania places a wreath of oak leaves on a monument shaped as the Iron Cross, stating « With pride, I have given a cherished head for the Fatherland ». (Private Collection)

of concentrated charges, the handling of explosives and smoke bombs, grenade throwing, estimating firing distances and so on. Theoretical lessons are dispensed in class rooms set up in the huts. Practical lessons take place on training grounds near the billets. Some are organised on a grand scale and against French positions opposite the divisional

sector. The French, who are aware of a training centre and used to its methods being tested against them, are constantly on their guard. A big party, where drink flows freely, closes the course before returning to units.

Michael asks to go and see a comrade from his company who is in a field hospital. He was hit by a shell splinter

The new model 1915 campaign uniform

A new campaign uniform was made official by order of the Imperial cabinet on 21 September 1915 and the decree of the 27 of the same month. The texts, applicable to Prussian units and the small states subordinate to the War Ministry, introduced modifications to the tunic, headwear and leather items. They were also put into place for Württemberg (10 October 1915), Saxony (9 November 1915) and Bavaria (31 March 1916)

The tunic was replaced by a model 1915 tunic (Bluse), designed to achieve simplification and standardisation. Carrying on with the uniformisation begun with the model 1907/10 uniform, it sim-

plified the distinction between service branches and was the same for other ranks and officers, except for the collar. The sewn down buttons securing the ends of the shoulder straps no longer carried the company number and were identical to those of the exterior pockets. The Bluse was really generalised in 1916 and at the beginning of 1917.

The trousers remained, in principle, fixed by the decree of 15 August 1914. However, the rapid deterioration of the trousers after a spell in the trenches and the lower quality cloth, rendered unnecessary a darker colour for the trousers as they were torn or worn out before the colour had time to fade. The decree of 14 November 1917 prescribed another model made of feld-grau cloth. In this way, a complete uniform could, in principle, be cut from the same piece of cloth, thereby avoiding a newly clothed soldier wearing a tunic and trousers of different shade. Another economy was achieved by abandoning the piping on the outside of the trouser legs.

The model 1915 greatcoat was made from the same cloth, with a green collar. When soldiers were issued with clothing that was too long, some cut of the bottoms and made puttees from them, but this wastage was punished. As for the shoulder straps, the decree of 9 July 1915 prescribed that they had to be sewn onto the clothing, the soldier attached his only pair on his tunic. An extra pair, often hastily made and without piping, was sometimes issued for the greatcoat. With the introduction of the Bluse, these articles sometimes underwent modifications.

The neck cloth was no longer part of the model 1915 uniform. As for the false bayonet knot, it slowly disappeared from the Front for various reasons.

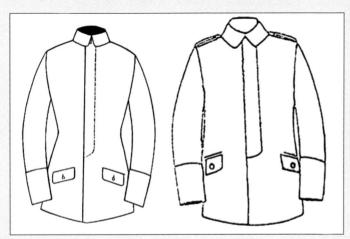

Model 1915 Bluse. Other ranks (right) officers (left). (P. Hesse Collection).

whilst acting as a front line runner. Michael is given a pass by his adjutant, with the agreement of his commander, that allows him a period of absence. He walks along the main road. At a crossroads, he is stopped by a *feldgendarme*, recognisable by his gorget hanging from a chain on his chest. When he arrives at the hospital he is told that his comrade has died. As it is late, the burial will take place the following morning. Back with his unit, he learns that, given the regimental programme, only the dead man's group will be present at the burial. This takes place in a cemetery opened near the hospital. The dead man is just clothed in his trousers and a flannel underwear, as stipulated by regulations and covered with a shroud, he is then lowered into the grave. Before being covered over, a nurse, a student in theology or a seminarian says a prayer. The pay book, identity tag and the man's personal items are sent to by the hospital administration to the company that he belonged to.

Michael's battalion goes back to the front lines. He shelters at night in an underground quarry situated in the second line. A few dozen prisoners arrive, the result of an action that took place a few hours previously. They are handed over to Michael's company who has to guard them for a while then escort them to the rear. Searching them is a source of mirth. Amidst loud laughing, the haul is commented on ; they find white bread, bars of chocolate, tins of sardines in oil, cake and cigarettes. Everything is shared out and the tins are opened with bayonets. A great meal begins, sardines and bread, cake and chocolate, and what's more, plenty of smokes ! The tunnels in this quarry are used to stock ammunition. Michael wonders how there have not been any serious accidents given that, every night, troops pass through this quarry, often sitting down for a rest and smoking a cigarette on crates of small arms ammunition, grenades, but also French gargousses (envelopes of gunpowder). Sometimes, in the columns of troops that come back from the front line, some soldiers continue to carry stick grenades from their belts with the pull string still hanging loose.

September 23 sees much activity within the regiment caused by transfers of men and materiel in view of creating a second machine gun company. Indeed, since the beginning of the year, the unit has had between 9 and 12 automatic weapons, including two or three captured examples. Having received extra supplies, this second company is created. A third will be formed later acting on a decision made on the previous 25 August. Each battalion then has its own machine gun company.

On the 24th, Michael hears rumours that the previous day's transfers were also the occasion to disperse a few junior NCOs of a company of his battalion other than his own. Indeed, they were treating their men badly, and the situation reached the ears of their hierarchy. The men in question formed a group that took rations destined for the men. Fresh meat, butter, sugar, potatoes and above all, beer, disappeared whilst the men had to make do with ordinary noodles, dried vegetables and tinned meat.

On the 25th, Michael is called to his company office. He has not yet had any leave, he can have 17 days, 14 of which for the leave itself and three for travelling. He is ordered to get his things ready and get on the *Feldbahn* that takes away the men going on leave to the village that houses the divisional headquarters. From there he has to take another train, an old local line, re-used for the needs of the German army, that arrives at the main billet area. He starts by going to the delousing building, then gets his leave pass stamped at the *Kommandantur*. As it is late, and he has a few hours to wait, he goes to the soldier's canteen to get a hot meal. Next, he finds a space on a normal train that takes him to the town of his regimental depot. Obviously, the journey lasts all night and some of the following day.

Michael is too tired to join in with the singing, games and carrying on of the other men going on leave at the same time as himself. He sleeps, opening his eyes from time to time when the train stops. The train seems to trundle along slowly given the speed limits that are imposed on it. Upon arrival in the large town where his old barracks are located, Michael has to fulfill a formality before taking the train which will take him to his journey's end. He presents himself at the Kommandantur to have his leave pass stamped. The NCO who stamps it takes him to the garrison major's office who gives him a severe dressing down for the state of his uniform. Michael explains, taking care to use the regulation terms and notably talking in the third person, that he has just come from the trenches. Listening to these

explanations only makes the officer more furious. « So you want to bring back your manners from the Front eh ? I'll have none of it ! Here, thank God, discipline reigns ». Changing his tone, he kindly tells Michael that he is going to send him to the clothing stores attached to his regimental depot. Michael shows his gratitude in the regulation way.

« Dismissed ! » says the officer. Michael bangs his heels together, salutes, does an about turn and goes. Armed with a document, he will be able to get a round field cap, tunic, neck cloth and trousers. They will not be new but at least in good condition. Their issue is noted down in Michael's pay book. He can now think about making his way to his family. He is going to take a train to his little town.

AUTUMN 1916.
MICHAEL IS WOUNDED

At the beginning of October, Michael sees the arrival of the new model 1915 tunics. They are worn by men who, after being wounded, have been re-clothed and reequipped with brand new items when returning to active service.

At the same time, he learns that his second brother has been called up. He has gone to the barracks where he himself had been mobilised, that is his regimental depot. He is going to undergo basic training for a few weeks and will then leave for the divisional recruit depot.

Salvage centre.
It is established in the line of communication area of each army. It functioned thanks to an army salvaged company. They collected together everything that was salvaged in the army zone, rags, old clothes, metals, bottles, recovered materiel or captured items and so on.
(Illustrierte Geschichte des Welkrieges 1914/16 Band IV)

A train ticket, issued by a unit for a soldier going on leave.
(P. Hesse Collection)

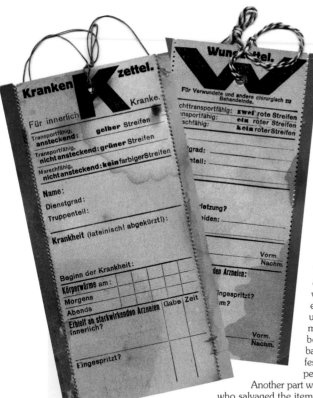

A label attached to a wounded man's greatcoat or tunic button (Wundzettel) or that of a sick man (Krankenzettel).
(J-C. Laparra Collection)

At this stage of the war, salvaging is in full swing. There are many orders read out on parade. Prescriptions are also broadcasted by other ways : posters inform the soldiers that if they salvage weapons such as, pistols, rifles, carbines and bayonets, as well as ammunition, belts, ammunition pouches, uniforms and brass, they will receive payment. These bonuses became attractive. Salvage operations were even organised within units when not on normal duty. Some of the bonuses were kept at battalion level to pay for festivities that took place periodically when at rest. Another part was paid out to the men who salvaged the items.

As explained on a note read on a report, « *Salvage bonuses are not a payment for voluntary work. On the contrary they should only be, for the troop and for each man, a stimulus that should prevent a duty, so important to the Fatherland, from being carried out negligently* ».

Individual and collective salvaging also continued as much as possible in the trenches. Michael himself takes a few risks. He sometimes crawls out of the trench. He finds abandoned tins of food to improve his rations, but he also collects copper drive bands from shells. The divisional salvage unit will give him a few pfennigs for each one. A rumour goes round that in some units, men have been severely punished for deliberately destroying ammunition to get the copper.

The issuing of uniforms during the war

It is difficult to evaluate the degree to which the need for clothing throughout the war was satisfied. It is a question of circumstances and the interpretation of soldiers' remarks. However, a shrewd observer can see that the uniformity of clothing and equipment in the German army did not exist. The latter never had the means to totally and rapidly issue its soldiers with uniforms and the different regulation models were never generalised. Also, after the appearance of each text introducing a new item of clothing, a period of tolerance was given so that the old clothing could be used up.

This situation created a diversity of models within units, aggravated by the existence of hastily made clothing made from bad quality cloth and sometimes of different shades. This mixture also resulted from the renovation of clothing which had its worn parts replaced by their good condition equivalents. In any case, it does not seem that the German army had, apart from a few critical moments (for example in the autumn of 1914 and in 1918), suffered from a lack of uniforms. However, they should not be too closely examined : they generally became of a detestable quality, shrinking when washed and only replaced when completely worn out.

In mid October, Michael hands his neck scarf in to the company quartermaster as it is worn to the thread and will not be replaced, as well as the false knot would around his bayonet frog that got caught in some barbed wire sticking out of a communication trench wall. When trying to pull it off, it tore and, when back in billets, could not be exchanged for one in good condition. On the other hand, he has been given a second pair of underpants as well as a woollen belt that will keep the cold off his stomach, thus avoiding intestinal problems. However, he has not been able to get any knee-heater only issued to some older men.

Everything points to an imminent return to the trenches. Extra field dressings are handed out, as well as a second ration of tinned meat and signalling flags for liaising with the artillery. The next day, the regiment attacks, with Michael's battalion in reserve. A runner arrives and informs the company commander that the battalion in front has taken two or three of the front line trenches. A light and scattered bombardment falls on the reserve battalion, particularly in front. A shout is passed along to the rear, « *Stretcher bearers forward !* ». There are, therefore, losses. Moving forward, Michael and his comrades soon pass the spot where the enemy shell landed. The victims have already been taken away. Bloody shreds of uniform and flesh hang from the tall grass and shrubs around the point of impact. A little further on, wounded men crouched down in a communication trench beg for water. Prisoners carrying stretchers make their way breathlessly to the rear, passing over the trenches to gain time.

Suddenly, there is a flash of light in front of Michael and a blow on his left thigh throws him to the ground. He thinks that he has been hit by a lump of earth, but hot blood running down his leg makes him realise that he has been wounded. He limps towards the closest trench where he collapses. Luckily, two stretcher-bearers come and place him on their stretcher, carrying him to a dugout where a dressing station in set up. Michael's equipment is taken off. He asks to keep his bread bag, water bottle and cup. An exhausted medical officer, standing in the middle of all the moaning bodies, cleans the wounds, injects an anti tetanus solution and tells the medical orderlies what to do. Tended, having received his injection, Michael is placed in a corner where he falls into a deep sleep. Several hours later, he is loaded, along with five other wounded men, into a horse drawn ambulance. One of them, suffering from horrendous wounds, sees the driver's pistol, hung along with the belt and bayonet on a post near him and begs the driver to put him out of his misery.

The ambulance arrives in a village. Michael is taken into the church that has been made into a triage area for the division's main aid post. His dressing is looked at and he is fed and given a drink, then he smokes a cigarette. He lays down on some straw, waiting to be moved. A medical orderly stops near Michael and explains that as his wound is light, that they believe he can manage a rail journey and there are many casualties, he certainly will not be going to a field hospital and possibly further to the rear into the line of communication area, into a permanent hospital. The bed available in these hospitals are no doubt going to be kept for men who are more seriously wounded than he is. He will surely be evacuated to Germany. He is taken to a muster point for the wounded and the sick at a station, then loaded onto a hospital train.

The following day, he arrives in a small town in the centre of Germany. He is transported to a garrison hospital now called a reserve hospital. During his stay in this establishment, he receives letters and cards from his family, friends and comrades. These are full of encouragement and are generally very patriotic.

As his wound does not require a long stay in a convalescent centre and he has not been laid up for too long,

Evacuation by rail

A hospital train stops in a station. The station building and the hotel and restaurant opposite have been turned into a muster point for the sick and wounded. The huts near the train are the annexe of a military hospital set up in the nearby village. (J-C. Laparra Collection)

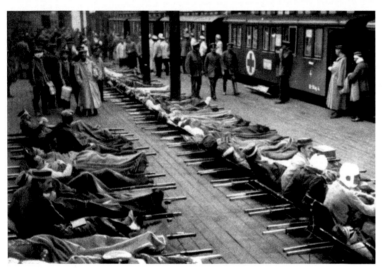

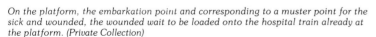

On the platform, the embarkation point and corresponding to a muster point for the sick and wounded, the wounded wait to be loaded onto the hospital train already at the platform. (Private Collection)

The interior of a hospital train carriage. (J-C. Laparra Collection)

Michael has to go to the divisional recruit depot without passing via the regimental depot and not even getting a short period of leave. However, getting back to the area behind the Front is not easy. Michael notes once again that the trains are late; the good personnel have been sent to the field railways; the coal is of poor quality, yet it has to be saved; brass pieces have been replaced by iron equivalents that do not perform in the same way. The trains, therefore, travel relatively slowly to reduce the wear on the rolling stock and avoid breakages.

Arriving at the divisional recruit depot, things move rather quickly! Michael is immediately sent to his regiment. When there, he sees his company pass by, to which as luck would have it, he is going to be sent back. The column moves slowly. The men's feet are covered in thick mud.

With muddy helmets, the rifle slung around their necks or across the stomach, the men march by with heads forward.

The lieutenant commanding the company supports himself with a walking stick. This is now a generalised trend, even amongst other ranks, men can often be seen wandering around with a club in hand. It is hard to believe that they are soldiers. They look strange with their helmets on and gas masks at the ready. The company is back from the trenches, the uniforms stiff with dry grey mud, the faces pale and eyes dull. Michael does not remember that a few weeks ago he looked the same. Images come back to him in flashbacks of the beginning of the war; the endless marches with his battalion with rigorously respected gaps maintained by the loud shouts of officers and NCOs, like

Morphine phials issued to German medical units. (Private Collection)

Aspects of the medical corps in Germany

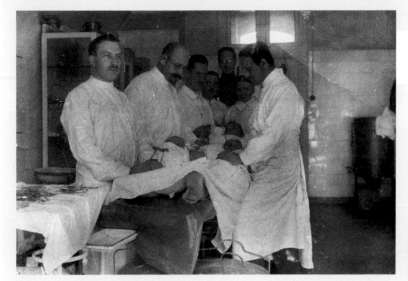

One of the operating theatres in a garrison hospital. (J-C. Laparra Collection)

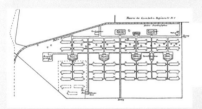

A map of a group of huts making up a hospital on military land. (J-C. Laparra Collection)

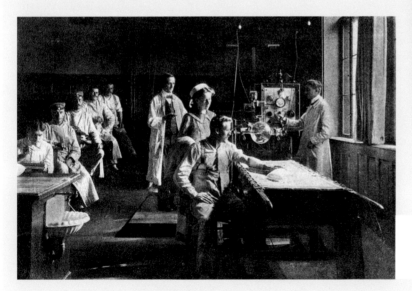

The number of pre-war garrison hospitals was not enough; other establishments had to be created by totally or partially requisitioning civilian hospitals, or in religious establishments, restaurants, theatres, or by purpose built groups of huts. (J-C. Laparra Collection)

A therapeutical X ray centre set up in a trade school transformed into a hospital. (P. Hesse Collection)

when on manoeuvres. At the time, in the regular regiments, the ranks were made up of young men, strong and baby faced, gleaming, washed, polished, with German cropped hair, freshly shaved and shining, at least at the beginning, with cleanliness and health, all or nearly all newly equipped and all proud! Michael notices also, that in his absence, his company has been issued with two large galvanised tin bottles or containers, called « tin haversacks » (Blechtornister) because they are effectively in the shape of a backpack (Tornister) and are worn with the backpack straps. They make it easier to bring water up to the front line on a daily basis.

1917.
WE HAVE TO HOLD ON IN THE WEST

In January, Michael's father, dispensed of his military obligations, is put into the civilian service, the auxiliary patriotic service, formed by the law of 5 December 1916. He can, however, carry on with his profession that is deemed useful for the German nation.

At the beginning of February, Michael's company is designated to go and reinforce a company of miners in the second position, in view of undertaking trench work. They have to make strong points. Indeed, they say that this sector is set up according to the latest directives. The defence is organised in depth, beginning with a forward zone where shell holes are permanently manned. The front line trenches, sometimes smashed by French heavy artillery bombardments, are now only considered as being shelter in calm periods.

Exceptionally, most of the move is done in trucks. When darkness falls, the order to depart is given. The men stand tightly packed together, nobody can sit. They bounce about to such an extent that they are nearly thrown out of the back of the trucks. The vehicles rumble along loudly and without lights. The roads are worn and full of potholes, the trucks have tireless wheels and are equipped with a replacement system.

The return of the victor. Postcard, published in 1915 and postmarked 29 October 1916. The sender is a certain Frieda who sends her warm greetings to the recipient. The card represents the victor returning home with a Russian prisoner hanging on the side of his pack. He is greeted by young girls that he knows who offer him flowers. On the side of his round cap, according to a tradition that could go back to the Duchy Wars (1848-1850 and 1864), he has put some oak leaves, the symbol of courage. (J-C. Laparra Collection)

At the side of a road linking different camps, a fountain is under construction by engineers in the shape of commemorative monument, hence the name « The pioneers' fountain » (1915). (Musées de la Cour d'Or, Metz)

Water, a precious resource for troops

A spring made in a trench. Miraculously it has not been disturbed by shellfire. It allows the occupants of neighbouring trenches to keep supplied with water. (Fr. Hervieux Collection)

In a village just behind the front lines, the occupants have added a monument to the communal fountain and called it the « barbarians' fountain » (1916). (J-C. Laparra Coll.)

A card wishing « warm Christmas greetings » and sent by an infantryman from Zossen camp, 20 December 1916. (J-C. Laparra Collection)

The convoy reaches the artillery lines. The gun pits are camouflaged with branches. The air is heavy with the smoke of the firing guns, the crashing sound echoing away. The company's most recent arrivals are strongly affected.

On 28 February, 12 light trench mortars (Minenwerfer) are shared out four to a battalion. The following night, Michael is designated to carry up the trench mortar ammunition. They have to carry up the projectiles from the dump near the engineer's divisional depot up to the mortars. The column of carriers strings out with huge gaps between each man to limit losses in the case of a bombardment. The itinerary taken passes by a portion known as the « path of death », which says much about what happens there sometimes.

On March 13, Michael is chosen to join a detachment made up of two machine guns groups that have to hold a company sector whilst the regiment pulls back during Operation Alberich, a withdrawal along part of the Front to the Siegfried Line ; all companies do the same. Each of the sectors previously occupied by the regiment will be covered by a patrol led by an officer. Before leaving, there is a religious service for those who wish to attend. The divisional chaplain has managed to borrow a specially equipped vehicle, a mobile field chapel. Given the circumstances, the service is brief. The villages through which the detachment passes through whilst moving up to the line, offer a mind-blowing sight. Whole companies break walls and roofs, pull down the support beams so that buildings collapse, cut down trees and fill in wells with whatever they can get their hands on. Right up to the Siegfried Line, each village is just a pile of ruins, each cellar that could be used as a shelter is blown up or rendered dangerous with booby traps. Every tree is cut down, every important crossroads cratered, every stream blocked by improvised dams, all cables are rolled up and taken away, all that can be burnt is torched. They have created a veritable desert.

Upon arriving in its combat trench, the detachment has to make its presence known in a realistic way in order to deceive the men opposite. This consists of making various noises, notably with mess tins, as if a full company is still in the trenches. Shovelled clods of earth are thrown over the parapet, rifles fired here and there along the length of the sector and a few rifle grenades launched without the help of a rack. Above all, they must find and push back enemy patrols that, having realised something is afoot, send more patrols to check the barbed wire defences. Finally, on the morning of the 17th, the last non booby-trapped dugouts are destroyed and the withdrawal is carried out rapidly, whilst enemy groups begin to press harder against the outposts.

Thanks to a letter brought by a man returning from leave, Michael learns that his brother, from whom he has not had any news for quite a while, is in a company of convalescent men that depend on his regimental recruit depot. He can, from time to time, get a short period of leave to go and see his parents. Previously part of another battalion within the regiment, he caught typhus and was sent to a

*Even though it was not in the front lines, this track was, however, a « Path of death ».
Der Weltkrieg im Bild. (Private Collection)*

A card with the postmark 5 January 1917, sent from the Eastern Front by an artilleryman to his brother who is in the infantry, thanking him for his Christmas card. A Mauser C96 pistol with its stock used as a holster can be seen on the man on the right who still wears a leather helmet with cover but with the ball removed. (J-C. Laparra Coll.)

The new defensive tactics.
These two photographs
were taken during a
demonstration organised
for leaders and the troop.
It is to show how to
organise the shell holes.

A hole organised more as
a station than for a combat
position.
(Illustrirte Zeitung N° 3884
6.Dezember 1917)

quarantine hospital where he nearly died. He is finding it
difficult to get over the illness. Classed as being fit for garrison duties only, he will not remain at the rear of the Front.
It is obvious that they are scraping the bottom of the barrel to find men and he knows that he will be sent to the
regiment's combat train. He will at least escape from going
into the front lines. Also, the brothers may get the chance
to meet up more easily when the regiment is at rest behind
the front lines.

April 24, a delousing session in a sunlit trench. Michael
notes that there are three sniper scopes in each company,
the men who have these scope-equipped rifles had passed
in front of Michael's dugout and he had a chat with them.
The delousing, where the funny side of the situation ends
up by generating a light hearted atmosphere, allows Michael
to finally learn the two verses of the « Louse song » and
its variation, « The louse hunt in Russian Poland ».
He heard them singing it but did not know the words very
well. These two songs are very popular among soldiers.
They are printed on postcards sold buy the cantine and
sent to Germany. Thus, they are well known there. Here
are three verses from the first song :

A hole transformed into a small post.
The men have helmets that have been
covered in earth to prevent them from
shining in the sun, bags of grenades under
their arms and pioneer shovels with
shortened handles.
(Illustrirte Zeitung No 3884 6.Dezember 1917)

A mobile field chapel.
With mobilisation, the army was equipped by religious
associations with a few Feldkapellenautos. These were
vehicles that allowed chaplains to go from billet to billet
and rapidly set up an altar.
The card is dated 18 February 1917.
(J-C. Laparra Collection)

*« In the middle of the black night, alone,
I begin the louse hunt.
I wonder whether the hardware store,
Has anything for these beastly lice.*

*We wake from sleep and launch the assault,
You sleep soundly in the night,
While we are louse-hunting.*

*How lucky you are to still be sleeping at home,
For you know nothing of our torment,
For us it is no shame.
We are louse-hunting for the fatherland.*

Hinter der Front.

Anton Magerfleisch
der Goulaschkoch.

The regiment was relieved yes-terday after two weeks spent in the trenches. It got back to the billets during the night. It is almost midday when the first men wake up, only because the smell of hot food is wafting through the air. Under a lean-to, the company field kitchen smokes away. Little by little, a queue grows in front of it, each man holding his mess tin.

At the front of the queue, the eternally hungry have been wai-ting for a long time. The two cooks are losing patience, the meal is ready and not all of the company is present. The men are asking them to start serving up the meals. « *Everyone must be here first* », says the healthy loo-king Unteroffizier cook.

He does not know, that after a relatively calm spell in the trenches, the last few hours were particularly difficult. The company was taken by surprise during the relief by an exceptionally heavy bombardment by the French artillery. Upon arriving at the billets, the roll call was only answered by 80 officers, NCOs and men instead of 130. The rations, therefore, are nearly double with meat, beans cooked in fat and more bread. The chewing-tobacco ration is of the same proportions, each man receiving 10 cigars, two cigarettes and two twists of tobacco. If it was not for the thought that so many rations were due to other men's suffering they could almost celebrate.

On May 16, Michael's company, along with every company in the regiment, is equipped with two model 1908/15 light machine guns. The crews are made up of a man in charge of the gun (an *Unteroffizier*), the gunner, a man to feed the gun (gunner's replacement) and two men to carry ammunition. This gun has been looked eagerly awaited; during the course of the previous month, there have been reinforcements from the divisional recruit depot with men who have been trained in the use of these guns.

During the month, three sets of trench armour plating have arrived in the company and placed in the platoons. When going to the section of front line trench next to his, Michael sees a sentry with the helmet brow plate, and also wearing the new trench armour. To his eyes it seems heavy and impractical.

The model 1908/15 light machine gun

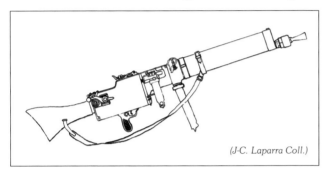

(J-C. Laparra Coll.)

The model 1908/15 light machine gun appeared in the spring of 1917. Taken from the model 1908 and equipped with a butt allowing the man operating it to fire using his shoulder and with a bipod, it was a formidable weapon. Its weight of 19.400 kg was obtained by taking away certain parts that were no longer indispensable. However, it was still water cooled (three litres in a water cooling jacket).

A machine gun crew. (J-C. Laparra Collection)

Model 1917 trench armour

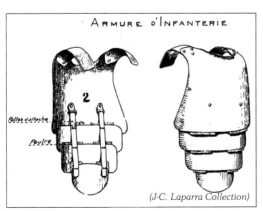

(J-C. Laparra Collection)

In October 1916, General Headquarters ordered the reprisal of experiments to be carried out for equipping infantry with armour.

The model 1917, made of tempered steel, weighed 8 to 10 kg and was painted grey. It comprised a breastplate, two shoulder plates and three lower protection plates.

It offered protection against shrapnel balls but not against rifle bullets fired from less than 500 metres away. It was effective for sentries and machine gunners. The first production examples (total production numbers are unknown) began arriving on the Western Front in May 1917. Considered as being trench equipment and not individually issued, this armour was unsuccessful because of its weight and the fact that it constricted movement.

A scene posed for the photographer showing the armour. Normally, the helmet should have been equipped with the brow plate. (P. Ramos Collection)

The Gaede helmet

The German High Command, looked at reducing losses, notably to head wounds, from an early stage, with the development of protective equipment.

The beginning of 1915 saw the appearance of a head protection known as the Gaede helmet, named after the general commanding the army in the Vosges and upper Alsace.

It was made under the impetus of lieutenant colonel Hesse, the detachment's chief of staff, and manufactured by the Mulhouse artillery workshops that produced approximately 1,500. It was made from a special steel and fixed by rivets onto a thick felt or leather head cover. It weighed more than 2 kg, was painted in a khaki colour and only protected part of the skull and face.

Destined more for sentries and considered as being position equipment, it was not issued on an individual basis.

Deutsche Kriegsausstellung Metz

Sonderausstellung des Kriegsmalers **Ernst Vollbehr**

The Gaede helmet as seen on one of the posters of the German War Exhibition organised by the Red Cross in Metz in May 1917 which included a one off exhibition by the war artist Ernst Vollbehr who was close to the Imperial Kronprinz. (Musées de la Cour d'Or, Metz)

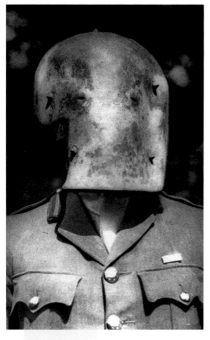

A German sniper's mask found by a Canadian soldier and worn by a British officer. (Le Miroir No 201 Sunday september 30 1917)

Michael is given an almost full month's leave, from June 18 to July 14, including travelling time. It has to be said that he has not had any for almost a year. During the journey home, he sees a poster in a station by the war artist, Vollbehr. It shows a Gaede helmet that he has never seen. On the other hand, he remembers having seen, after a spell in another regiment the previous month, a sort of armoured shield behind which was a sniper, peering out across the parapet.

On July 15, Michael rejoins his regiment that is at rest once more. At the evening parade, the company adjutant announces that an order has been given for all men from the Empire Lands of the Alsace Lorraine, with no German ancestry and serving on the Western Front, to be sent to units serving on the Eastern Front (Russia and Rumania), within nine days.

Michael and his comrades bid farewell to two Lorraine comrades from their platoon, one young and the other old. They were great comrades and at times full of fun. However, the words « traitor » and « deserter » were often aimed at them by NCOs who were wary of them. It is true that some men of the Lorraine do not hide their disgust at serving in the German uniform, calling themselves « Muss-Preusse » (in French, « Malgré nous », meaning literally « in spite of our will » but in German « I must be Prussian »).

The following day, 150 Alsace Lorraine men of the regiment, who fall under this measure, are grouped together

whilst the companies gather for morning roll call. Quickly and silently, the detachment is led to the station. Michael learns later that a first departure of 2,000 men from the Alsace Lorraine was organised on the 16th at the main station of the lines of communication area. These men were put onto five trains that took them to their initial destination of Brest Litovsk, in Bielorussia. They say that as the trains left one by one, the men on the trains sang the « March of Lorraine ».

On August 3, the regiment goes back to the trenches. Firstly they have to take the roads behind the lines. The order to sing having been given, the men have to sing the usual assortment of songs at the top of their voices. For a change, a man at the head of the battalion has the idea of singing the popular « Chimney sweep » song :

« Young nuns, rejoice.
Tomorrow we will sweep your chimneys,
Sweep, sweep ! »

As soon as he hears the first verse, an adjutant tries to intervene and forbid this « filth ». The captain in command of the battalion indicates that they can continue and the column carries on:

« Sister Clara prefers to see
Every man's brush,
Sweep, sweep ! »
Etc.

A new stay in the trenches begins badly. Men arrive, wearing breeches with leather pads on the knees and the seat, special boots and puttees, identifying them as grenade men from an assault unit. The news soon spreads from dugout to dugout that something nasty is going to happen. The general image of these men is that for an attack, they arrive early, having been brought up by truck from their billets far behind the front lines to the second line positions.

They assault the enemy after a short artillery barrage, sometimes taking with them shock groups from the unit holding the sector, bring back a few prisoners then return to the rear. As for the ordinary infantry men, they remain

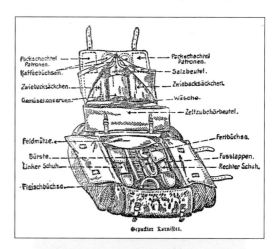

The contents of the backpack circa 1917.
In a U shape around the backpack is the tent section and blanket. The flap holds two boxes of ammunition, two boxes of coffee, two boxes of war biscuits, a tin of vegetables and linen. The main compartment holds the folded round cap, left boot, brush, tin of grease, Russian socks, tin of meat, right boot.
(P. Hesse Collection)

The men of Lorraine in Russian Poland (1917)

4 February, infantry men, too old to be recruits, no doubt men of the Landwehr given their appearance. These were men usually put into units stationed in the East. The board says that they are « Joyous men of the Lorraine » and also says « Who knows if we'll come back ». Note the six model 1898 rifles including two with model 1898/05 bayonets, model 1909 ammunition pouches, blackened leather and boots and feldgrau trousers. There are, on the other hand, items of clothing and equipment that was being replaced or that had already been deleted in certain units; model 1907/10 tunics, corduroy trousers, brass belt buckles, spiked helmets (a model 1895 in varnished black leather, six Ersatz felt helmets with brass or coppered metal fittings). The pack worn by the man kneeling on the left does not appear to be a regulation backpack.
(J-C. Laparra Collection)

Summer. Camille and another « Muss-Preusse » from the region of Hagondange, serving in the same regiment for the duration of the war on the Eastern Front. On the left, Camille wears a model 1907/10 tunic (Feldrock) without the neck cloth, and a round cap with removable model 1915 band. On the right, his compatriot wears a round cap that is no doubt already the model 1917. He has a model 1915 tunic (Bluse), completed with a neck cloth that is not, in principle, worn with this garment. (J-C. Laparra Coll.)

in their lines and are bombarded all day as a reprisal for the attack; by the evening there are only a handful of men left.

The men of assault troops are celebrated, mentioned in despatches, given medals and receive preferential treatment. This time, the men with the leather pads have only come to reconnoitre an eventual departure point for a future operation.

A new relief. The battalions billet in three neighbouring villages. In Michael's village, new war bond posters have been stuck up. The following day is given over to chores such as cleaning, improving the billets then various parades, cleaning and inspection of rifles and checking the contents of haversacks, boot inspection etc.

The 5 September is declared a rest day; at the morning parade, the company adjutant reads out a service note signed by the commander of the regiment. Officers, NCOs and soldiers are strongly encouraged to participate in the

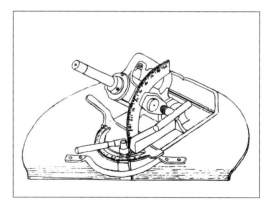

The Model 1916 grenade launcher on its platform. (J-C. Laparra Collection)

On the left. The Model 1916 grenade launcher and its projectile. The man takes aim. (Illustrirte Zeitung No 3884 6.Dezember 1917)

Helft uns siegen!

zeichnet Kriegsanleihe

A propaganda postcard
(postmarked 26 October
1917) « Help us win! Buy
war bonds ».
(J-C. Laparra Collection)

Nützet Euch,
nützet dem Vaterland,
zeichnet Kriegsanleihe

Newspaper adverts inciting
to buy war bonds.
(Illustrirte Zeitung
Kriegsnummer 165
27.September 1917)

war effort and to buy war bond stamps as part of the current war bond drive. During the day the men receive booster inoculations against cholera. The following day, he receives a postcard sent by his family which is also on the theme of war bonds. Decidedly, the propaganda is going all out.

The regiment returns to the line on the 13th. On the 28th, Michael learns that the grenade launcher *(Granatenwerfer)* platoons have been disbanded. He notices, shortly after, that the equipment is shared out with two

In a village less than ten kilometres behind the front lines, a war bond poster above a road sign.
(J-C. Laparra Collection)

launchers per company. On October 1, he notices again that the number of light machine guns per company is now four.

On this day, a gas mask inspection is carried out by the regimental gas officer. The latter changes those with defects for a new model where the rubberised cloth is replaced by soft leather *(Lederschutzmaske)*.

After a spell in the second line positions where they were put to work improving the positions, Michael's battalion is relieved and goes to a village just behind the Front. He has

to take part in a raid with some of the divisional pioneer company and some other outside reinforcements, two groups from an army assault battalion with a few pioneers specialised in the handling of flame throwers. The assault grenadiers, apparently 16 in all, are rather tall, well built and wearing clean uniforms, ; nearly all of them have the Iron Cross Second Class. T

he flame thrower men are nothing special, even though they are considered as being elite troops ; they wear no particular clothing. However, most wear a simple insignia on their left forearm bearing a small death's head indicating that they are part of the « *Totenkopf Pioniere* » (Death's head pioneers : the reserve pioneer regiment of the Prussian Guard).

Some « *Schipper* » an untranslatable term designating men from a labour battalion, bring up two flame throwers with circular tanks, on carts for the pioneers. They unload them very carefully.

Michael's company arrives and what a contrast they are. The infantrymen seem crushed with fatigue and march bent over, wearing the round cap, their helmets hanging by the chinstrap on a forearm. Some of them have puttees but most wear boots. Some of them march with the aid of a stick. The tunics are filthy, patched up, worn and faded. The faces are pale and thin ; many have a few days growth of beard.

The training will last a week. Training area has been set aside near the camp, it comprises of perfect trenches with dugouts, nice straight traverses, communication trenches and a network of barbed wire. Friendly and enemy lines are well represented, with their exact positions, so they say. A company of « Schipper » have built the practice trenches under the supervision of their superiors. At the end of this period of exercises, the men are given a day of rest. Later, the men take up their positions during the night, the raid itself is not described.

There is a new relief. At the morning parade, Michael learns that he has been awarded the Iron Cross Second Class. He is not fooled and knows that no particular action can be attributed to him during the operations in which his company has participated. He has undergone an assault training course and since, participated from time to time in patrols, being lucky enough to come through them unscathed. Above all, he has been part of the same company since the beginning of the war and that is rare enough in itself. As well as this, he has never been punished. At the next parade, the company is assembled in its usual place.

« *Company. Attention! Eyes right!* » orders the adjutant. The company remains still. With a steady step, smartly dressed in his usual service uniform, the lieutenant comes

The leather gas mask

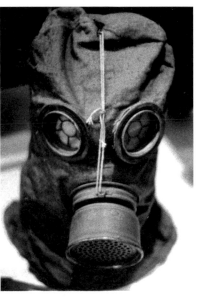

The box for storing the protective hood for wounded men.
(J-C. Laparra Collection)

The standard Model 1917 gas mask. The one shown here does not have the string that links the plate to the upper strap.
(J-C. Laparra Collection)

The gas mask for the wounded. The string is to ensure the weight of the filter is evenly distributed for the whole mask.
(J-C. Laparra Collection)

After the introduction of leather gas masks, issued from June 1917 onwards, the rubberised cloth models were not taken back. Due to a low production rate of the leather model, they were changed progressively. At the beginning, they were reserved for front line troops. In November, the generalisation was well advanced. This mask was slightly modified and the corresponding production was launched in October 1918. Note that a mask for wounded men, incapable of putting on or adjusting their masks, was seen in August 1918. This was a protective hood which used elements of the Lederschutzmaske.

The order of the Iron Cross

The Iron Cross Second Class with combatant's ribbon.
(Private Collection)

The order of the Iron Cross, created in 1813 and used again in 1870, was brought back into use by Wilhelm II on 5 August 1914.

From 2 September, the Kaiser delegated the award of the Iron Cross Second Class to generals in service.

This medal comprised four classes of which the 2nd was really the medal for German NCOs and privates.

Rare at the beginning of the war, it became common in 1916 and even more so in 1918. Awards of this medal were still considered from 1919 to 1925.

An award certificate for the Iron Cross Second Class. This sort of document was usually signed, by a delegated officer, in the name of the recipient's unit commander.
(Reproduced with the permission of Mrs M.-H. Bowman).

Prost !
*In front of the canteen (Kantine), some stretcher bearers or nurses, including a man of rank, drink from their beer mugs. Five have the Iron Cross, three in the form of a chest pin (authorised for NCOs and privates since 29 August 1916) on the left side of the breast, two are in the form of an apparently new ribbon, put through one buttonhole. They are perhaps celebrating the latter two's recent award of the medal ? Before each round, the traditional formula is pronounced « Prost ! » (the popular abbreviation for prosit, good health).
(J-C. Laparra Collection)*

the evening, Michael takes a few comrades to the canteen for the traditional celebrations.

At this time, Michael sees within the reinforcements, young men wearing a new « head scratcher ». Out of curiosity, he asks a comrade in the battalion staff about it. He learns that, by a decree dated 20 July 1917, the field cap has been replaced by standard model for all service branches with a green band and piping. The replacement will depend on availability. For the time being, none have arrived within the regiment to replace the old model.

SPRING 1918.
THE FINAL PUSH,
SO THEY SAY !

Michael receives a letter dated at the end of December informing him that his sister has been incorporated into the Patriotic Auxiliary Service. From June 1917, single women aged between 20 and 40 have been employed within different army services, including the general governments of Belgium and Poland, and even within billeting areas. She is going to Belgium where she will work as a washer woman in a military hospital.

For January, Michael has turned a few pages into a glossary. He notes the special language that is used by front line soldiers. Bread is « a simple square », a shelter is a « storage room », a plane bomb is « gingerbread », to be wounded is « to get one », to be bombed is « to be watered », the telephone line is « the chatting line », the billet soldiers are « the billet pigs », a decoration « tinplate » or « plumbingé », a light wound is « a ticket home », a safe occupation is a « cushy number », etc.

Time drags on in the trench and there is not much to talk about. Michael has also noted down the remarks of comrades concerning the evolution in personal equipment since 1914. The neck cloth has disappeared, there has

out of his office, passes in front of the ranks and stands opposite the troops. He has a paper in his hand. The adjutant carries on. « *Rifleman Michael, 30 paces forward. Quick march !* »

In his black boots that he has had to polish to make them shine, Michael marches out, his arms slightly held to his sides and halts after 30 paces to the left of the company commander who begins speaking. « *In the name of his majesty the Emperor, the general commanding the division has awarded the Iron Cross Second Class to Musketeer Michael. I give you my hearty congratulations !* »

The lieutenant approaches Michael and opens a small blue packet and pulls a black and white ribbon through a buttonhole from which hangs the cross. The adjutant says « *About turn !* » Michael turns and goes back to his place. He is sweating from the emotion of it all ; luckily his trousers are baggy and hide his trembling knees. Naturally, in

A farm transformed into a camp (November 1917) The buildings are occupied and huts built nearby. (Private Collection)

been another pair of underwear since 1916, initially there were two shirts, now when one is worn out, they have to wait a long time for it to be replaced and as very often there is only one, the woolen belt distributed in 1916 has not been renewed when worn out. Two pairs of socks are now one and it is better to make a pair of foot bindings when possible. The issue of a pair of boots along with strong lace up shoes has now perhaps passed to a pair of boots or ankle boots with puttees from 1917 onwards. They had one blanket (two in winter) and now there is only one for all seasons in 1918. On the other hand, they have had two water bottles since 1916.

In mid January, there is talk of a relief and a move to the rear for training. On the 19th, the regiment is relieved at four in the morning. The men march off in a heavy snow storm to a village where they think they will be picked up by trucks. They are to be disappointed, however. Times are hard and trucks and petrol have to be economised. They have to carry on marching through most of the day.

Finally, the regiment arrives at its destination. It will be billeted in an area for a certain period in order to prepare for a future great offensive. This rural location, as is the case with all those around, is full of soldiers, including barns, attics, churches and schools. As for the surrounding countryside, it has been transformed into training areas, firing ranges and specialised polygons.

Firstly, the regiment, like others, has received the highest number of recruits for many years from the divisional depot. The units practice firing with different weapons and perfect hand grenade throwing as well as rifle grenades, repeating the different forms of almost forgotten combat techniques of open warfare.

Formations undergoing training are so closely packed together that sometimes bullets buzz over the heads of the men. One day, a man from Michael's company operating a light machine gun hits the commander of another regiment on horseback whilst he was evaluating an exercise in front of his officers. Luckily he got away with a light shoulder wound. On two or three occasions, Michael's company carries out practice attacks with live ammunition on trench systems where the enemy is represented by targets. The object is to put to use the experience gained by the regiment in the great battle of November 1917. Here also, men are wounded. On one occasion they even undertake, down to the slightest detail, manoeuvres organised on a divisional level. A large scale attack is simulated, with an assault behind a creeping barrage marked by red flags. This is a rehearsal, even if the progression is several kilometres deep, against positions marked out with white tapes that correspond to real objectives that are only known to officers.

On 1 February, the number of light machine guns per company changes to six, they need two carts to transport these weapons and their ammunition.

The model 1917 rifle grenade cup

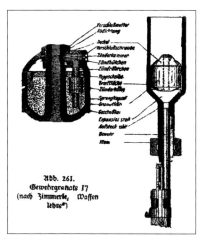

Abb. 261. Gewehrgranate 17 (nach Zimmerle, Waffen lehre*)

The cup that fitted to the end of the rifle and a grenade, both taken from the French Vivien Bessiere system, were introduced in the winter of 1917/18. They replaced the model 1913 and 1914 grenades with rod.

Seen for the first time in November 1917, they were generalised from 24 April 1918, being initially issued four to a company in attack divisions.

With a range of 150 metres, the projectile weighed 445 grams of which 35 was the explosive.

(Fr. Sesselberg, Der Stellungskrieg 1914-1918, 1926)

Towards the end of the month, Michael's regiment is taken to billets not too far from the front line. Training is not over ; after several exercises at battalion and company level, they rehearse on two occasions, on a huge position indicated by white tapes, a penetration by the whole division. The general commanding the latter next gives a pep talk to the assembled unit. Those that can hear him realise that the attack will take place in the next few days and that it will be the final push that will break the Entente.

After a spell in the trenches in a quiet sector, it is an almost complete regiment that finds itself at rest. On 15 March, the regimental signals detachment is organised into four platoons, one for the staff and one per battalion. Given his length of service, Michael is promoted to Corporal. He sews a button indicating his rank on each side of his collar. He is also transferred to the company

Field Marshal Hindenburg inspecting a division

Beginning of February 1918, a large unit at rest and in training behind the front lines. The field marshal, chief of the general staff of the army on campaign, is accompanied by the state sovereign to which the division belongs. After a tactical demonstration there is a parade.

The arrival of the authorities on the ground where a parade awaits. (J-C. Laparra Collection)

The troops on parade. (J-C. Laparra Collection)

The march past by one of the division's regiments. The first battalion with, in succession, the major commanding the first battalion, the lieutenant chief of the 1st company, the officer candidate whose platoon makes up the front ranks. (J-C. Laparra Collection)

command group where he is put in charge of its runners. Michael takes the opportunity to ask for a certificate proving his wound so that he can buy the new wound badge from the regimental canteen.

On 18 March, the regiment leaves the billets after the evening meal. Firstly, it marches to a chateau in the Somme where it remains until the following evening. The staffs of the regiment and the battalions, as well as the services of one or two companies are billeted in the chateau itself and its outbuildings, the men being forbidden to light fires in the stoves and fireplaces. The rest of the regiment bivouacs nearby despite the bad weather conditions and they are also forbidden to light fires. When night falls they

continue their march. Sentries at bridges make sure that all that is superfluous is left behind.

When day breaks, the regiment disappears into the deep dugouts in a large shell cratered field, not far from the village. Next, on the third night, the regiment snakes its way through communication trenches to the front lines. Here, near a devastated village, they relieve a unit. They say that the front line trench forms a sharp angle that is known as the « salient » on the trench map covering the sector. The artillery preparation begins at 04.40 hrs and is of an unpre-

Unser täglich Brot gib uns heute
Brotkarte
Berlin und Nachbarorte
XXXIII   33836
Du sättigst alles   was da lebet
Erinnerung an eiserne Zeit

At the rear too, times are hard !
A propaganda postcard published « as a souvenir of the iron era » and showing a bread ration card for Berlin and the surrounding area. It incites people to make do with what is distributed, even using religion to this end : « Lord give us this day our daily bread… You satisfy all who live here » This did nothing for the morale of the men at the Front when they received this card ! This example is postmarked 9 February 1918.
(J-C. Laparra Collection)

The wound badge

Adopted on the order of the Emperor's cabinet on 3 March 1918, it was made of iron and represented a steel helmet with crossed swords, surrounded by a crown of laurels. It was in black for one or two wounds, silver for three or four and gold for five or more. It was worn on the lower left hand side of the chest, above the belt.

The wound badge for one or two wounds.
(P. Hesse Collection)

A wound badge certificate.
(J. Didier Collection)

Dem Gefr. Raf. Karl Beier
6. Komp. Reserve-Infanterie-Regiments 258
habe ich heute das
Abzeichen
für einmalige Verwundung
verliehen
Im Felde, den 5. Mai 191 8.
Oberstleutnant u. Reg. Kommandeur

Druckerei C. Appelhans & Comp. (Red. Stolle & Guß. Rotelied), Braunschweig.

An NCO with the wound badge on his model 1915 tunic. He also has two medals, including the Iron Cross Second Class. Judging from the visible shoulder strap, he is part of a Württemberg infantry regiment. However, on the left side of his cap he wears an Edelweiss, the symbol of the Alpine Corps. Perhaps he was wounded or no longer fit for the mountains and drafted into a normal regiment. (J-C. Laparra Collection)

1

Officers, NCOs and soldiers « visit » an old British camp (April 1918). (J-C. Laparra Collection)

On 21 March or the days just after, behind the Allied lines, fighting men or men moving up loot a train loaded with supplies. (Der Weltkrieg im Bild, 1926)

cedented magnitude. At 06.40 hrs, judging from the sound of the shells hurtling overhead, the infantrymen feel that the bombardment has reached its peak.

At 09.00 hrs, the infantry receives the order to go over the top and to take up assault positions by going through the enemy counter barrage. Four and half hours after the beginning of a barrage of unprecedented proportions, and half an hour after the first reconnaissance patrols, the attacking troops leave their positions and begin moving forward behind their creeping barrage, taking care that the curtain of shell fire falls in front of them. This preparatory movement is helped by a thick morning fog.

At 09.39 hrs, the creeping barrage begins to fall and Michael sees demolition squads advance in order to place Bangalore torpedoes under the wire that has not been destroyed by the bombardment.

At 09.40 hrs, when the latter explode, the soldiers of the assault units, accompanied by pioneers get up and taking the infantrymen with them, go through the wire destroyed by the creeping barrage.

Following his company commander, Michael sees the men around him manoeuvre as riflemen under the command of their officers and NCOs. These groups move forward without worrying about centres of resistance that will be dealt with by mopping up units. The advance continues taking advantage of dead ground, valleys, ravines and sunken roads, as well as what is left of woods.

In a valley, already well behind the enemy lines, Michael's company comes across an old British camp ; it is deserted but still completely equipped with furniture, camp equipment and beds, clothing and even personal items. This causes a stampede. Nobody commands any more. The desire to loot is greater and more widespread than drunkenness caused by wine. This is caused by the incredible frustration born of years of going without and the feeling that they have been hoodwinked by the government and the high command.

SUMMER - AUTUMN 1918. IT'S THE END...

After the « final push », there are other offensives, including that of July that is supposed to bring about peace, the « *Friedensturm* ». After its failure, the troops take up new positions along the Aisne and Vesle rivers. The final waves of the Allied counter offensive break against them and later retire. Fighting breaks out in certain areas, then things calm down once more. Michael has heard that many German divisions, exhausted and in need of refitting, have been sent to rest at the rear. Some of them are billeted around the small town of Avesnes where the chief quarter-master general, General Ludendorff, has set up his command post. The latter, along with the chief of the general staff of the campaign army, field marshal Hindenburg, have to inspect the division.

In the billets, the regiment furiously cleans itself up. All of the men are inspected by their officers; any torn clothing is replaced for similar items in good condition. Michael gets a new tunic and one of his comrades gets a whole set of new equipment. When the generals leave, the old worn out items are given back to their owners. The new clothing or equipment was just to make a good impression during the inspection.

Michael, when watching his comrades, realises how quickly his men recover their strength. If they can sleep for days on end, they forget, or so it seems, all the terrible things they have been through. However, to fully recover, they need a real rest, far from enemy shells or bombs, and if possible, far enough away not to hear the guns. Unluckily, real rest periods are rare and very short for troops. Moved from sector to sector, they remain under an almost constant mental and physical duress.

July 30 sees a relief and billets in a village. The night, and those after it, are clear and favourise the visits by Allied aircraft that bomb strategic areas. After a day of rest and despite the situation, the everyday life behind the lines carries on with exercises, all sorts of lessons, roll calls and inspections taking up most of the days spent far from the front lines. Supplies are, once more, not very bountiful and of a mediocre quality. During this period, the daytime ration comprises only of cucumbers that end up being called « gardener's sausages ».

Back in the trenches in a sector that is relatively unmarked by the war, Michael's battalion has to launch an almost immediate attack after an artillery preparation lasting half

German prisoners, summer 1918.
Escorted by guards, they make their way to the rear, helping the wounded and carrying captured materiel such as a model 1908/15 light machine gun on the right. One of the prisoners wears a camouflaged Stahlhelm.
(Le Miroir No 252 Sunday 22 September 1918)

Schulz bei Fliegerangriff im Keller hinter diesem Hause.

Schulz bei Fliegerangriff hier im Stollen

A sign showing the position of shelters to be used during an attack from the air.
(M. Talfournier Collection)

A visit by Wilhelm II during the summer of 1918

After having walked through some streets, the Emperor decorates with the Iron Cross some recipients, gathered at a street corner. (Morhange municipal Archives)

A parade in the market place.
(Morhange municipal Archives)

An example of a leaflet dropped over German lines

Destined for German soldiers, it showed that the United States had entered the war with all their power on the side of the Allies, not against the German people, but against the government and the ruling classes that exploited them. This American intervention is the result of this government's politics. The document is printed on both sides and encourages German soldiers to give themselves up to the Allies where they will be well fed, looked after and treated as brave men. (J. Didier Collection)

Evoking the favourable position towards making peace by the social democrat newspaper « Vorwärts » and the conditions within Germany, the leaflet seeks to convince that « this peace will not be peace, not peace that feeds, it will be hell on earth, even more ferocious than the war ». *It exhorts soldiers, therefore, to* « hold the Western Front ». (J-C. Laparra Collection)

an hour. The company commander gives his orders to the platoon leaders. « Groups in columns of one, with intervals of twenty metres. The markers are the trees behind which is the village we have to take ». A favourable indication of the morale that reigns within the rank and file is that he has to designate a man to remain behind to point the field kitchen in the right direction; no one wanted to volunteer for this task. Michael marches behind the company commander who, using his stick, sometimes signals to the platoon leaders to change pace or rectify the formation of their platoons. The smoke of many shell bursts drifts across the edge of the village towards which the company advances.

On September 4, the battalion *Minenwerfer* platoon is disbanded; the men and materiel of the platoons of the three battalions now make up a regimental company.

On September 20, Michael's division is at rest near a small town in the annexed region of the Lorraine. He sees the Emperor pass by with his entourage, all with shining boots, impeccable and rutilant uniforms covered with numerous medals and braid and the now old fashioned spiked helmets with covers. An officer seems to have come from another world, an old man with a long moustache, ridiculous in his Guard's Hussars colback.

Michael is surprised at the difference between these characters, surrounding the « warlord » who people say is a shadow of his former self, and the rifleless men lined up along the pavements. All this decorum given the German army's situation on the Western Front! At the same time, morale was even

A missing soldier (a ravine north east of Verdun, 1968) (J-C. Laparra Collection)

lower as despite being forbidden, the men pick up the leaflets that manage to find their way to the soldiers. These leaflets that exist in different formats, incite the soldiers to desert to the other side where they will be well treated and fed. A 30 pfennig reward per leaflet proves that the high command takes them seriously. It should be added that this money is taken from the populations of the occupied territories.

At the same time, news of interior politics reaches their ears through men that arrive from Germany for various reasons and bring with them pamphlets and newspapers.

On 21 October, Michael notes that his regiment's battalions have been reformed with three companies instead of four. He has heard that they cannot count on receiving any reinforcements. After a short rest, with the guns rumbling in the distance, they have to go back to the front lines.

This is the final entry in the last notebook. There is nothing that enables us to know the fate of its owner and how it came to be reunited with the other notebooks.

MICHAEL, FROM THE HERD INSTINCT TO RESIGNATION

Michael was part of a war machine that was often preceded by a favourable reputation. This no doubt largely came from the pre war situation of its regular soldiers, with their impeccably smart uniforms, strong discipline, efficient organisation, quality equipment in plentiful supply etc.

When hostilities broke out, the German army had been modernising for several years. There were new uniforms, equipment, weapons and so on. The operation, that mostly concerned regular units, in accordance with the mobilisation plans, meant that that the invasion forces in 1914, were a remarkable sight overall. An effort to modernise was kept up throughout the war, adapting to new requirements, in particular tactically, and economic constraints.

The needs of the army during the conflict appear to have been covered thanks to a reasonable organisation and an absolutely total mobilisation. When we glance at Michael's living condition, we see that men and units had all that they needed. However, there were times when they lacked things that make up a soldier's environment. Apart from when he received a good condition backpack to go into the front lines or when part of a parade inspected by high ranking officers, Michael was often badly clothed and equipped. His food become progressively worse and dull. He also knew that his family was suffering from hunger at home.

It was a long time since the time when Germany, sure of victory, saw Michael with a small bunch of flowers hanging from a buttonhole paraded through the streets of his garrison town. He no doubt thought, as did his comrades,

The war memorial at Endingen, north west of Fribourg-en-Brisgau (2002) It represents George slaying the dragon, one of the themes of commemorative statues in the catholic regions of Germany. The perfect example of knightly values and the patron saint of all knights in Christendom, Saint George is notably the protector of the Teutonic knights. The symbol of faith and righteous strength, slaying the devil (evil) represented by the dragon with the help of God, he defends the weak and those who are in danger.
(J-C. Laparra Collection)

that he had become a « frontschwein », literally a front line pig. Although he maintained his sense of duty, still feeling bound by the oath made on the flag when he was still a recruit in 1911, he wondered about the future of the Empire. Amongst the men around him, some crossed the line as far as discipline was concerned, and did all they could to avoid following orders or prolonged their periods of leave without permission. Others went to the extreme of deserting within Germany or to the enemy.

At the end of October, Michael, scrupulous and resigned to his fate, no doubt did his duty to the end, but we do not know when or how his war ended.

One of the two monuments in the German military cemetery of Piennes (2007). This group, representing a consoling Christ aiding a dying soldier was made by the sculptor, E.Raspe of Cologne, who was serving with the 30th Siege Engineers Column.
(P. Hesse Collection)

ACKNOWLEDGEMENTS

J.-L. Baur, M. H. Bowman, J. Didier, R. Heit, Fr. Hervieux, (Col. Ret.) R. Kopp, (Maj. Ret.), N. Kugel, A. Laparra, J. Laparra, (Col. Ret.) G. Ozenne, P. Gérardin, (Col. Ret.) X. Pierson and L. Remy (Manager and librarian/researcher, Mémorial de Verdun, Fleury-devant-Douaumont), H. Plote, M. Prévôt (administrative manager, town hall Morhange), P. Ramos, E. Siegel, M. Sublet, (Capt. Ret.) M. Talfournier.

« I had a comrade.. » *(Private Collection)*

RECOMMENDED READING

BEUMELBURG W.,	*Combattants allemands à Verdun. Payot, 1934.*
ETTIGHOFFER P. C.,	*Verdun Opération Jugement. Éditions France-Empire, 1964.*
JOHANNSEN E.,	*Quatre de l'infanterie. Éditions de l'Épi, 1929.*
JÜNGER E.,	*Orages d'acier, Journal de guerre. Christian Bourgois éditeur, 1970.*
KLING Recteur,	*Le 122ᵉ Régiment d'Infanterie de Landwehr dans la guerre mondiale. Traduction commentée et préface de J-C. LAPARRA. Culture et Loisirs, 1996.*
LAPARRA J-C.,	*Les « Gladiateurs ». Des grenadiers aux divisions d'attaque. Les formations offensives dans l'armée allemande 1914-1918. Ysec éditions, 2007.*
LAPARRA J-C.,	*La grande débrouille. Un point de vue iconoclaste sur l'armée allemande 1914-1918. Ysec éditions, 2005.*
LAPARRA J.-C., DIDIER J., HESSE P.,	*La machine à vaincre. De l'espoir à la désillusion. Histoire de l'armée allemande 1914-1918. Éditions 14-18, 2006.*
LAPARRA J-C., HESSE P.,	*Les chemins de la souffrance. Le service de santé allemand Saint-Mihiel - Hauts-de Meuse - Woëvre - Metz 1914-1918. Ysec éditions, 2003.*
REMARQUE E. M.,	*À l'Ouest rien de nouveau. Stock 1929/Le Livre de poche 1962.*
RENN L.,	*Guerre. Ernest Flammarion, 1929.*
RICHERT D.,	*Cahiers d'un survivant. Un soldat dans l'Europe en guerre 1914-1918. La Nuée Bleue, 1994.*
UNRUH Fr. von,	*Verdun. Éditions du Sagittaire, 1924.*
VAN DER MEERSCH M.,	*Invasion 14. Albin Michel 1935/Le Livre de poche 1965.*
ZWEIG A.,	*L'éducation héroïque devant Verdun. Librairie Plon, 1938.*

A publication